DATE DUE

EDUCATE, Medicate, or Litigate?

Robert C. DiGiulio

EDUCATE, Medicate, or Litigate?

**What Teachers, Parents, and Administrators
Must Do About Student Behavior**

CORWIN PRESS, INC.
A Sage Publications Company
Thousand Oaks, California

For information:

Corwin Press, Inc.
A Sage Publications Company
2455 Teller Road
Thousand Oaks, California 91320
E-mail: order@corwinpress.com

Sage Publications Ltd.
6 Bonhill Street
London EC2A 4PU
United Kingdom

Sage Publications India Pvt. Ltd.
M-32 Market
Greater Kailash I
New Delhi 110 048 India

Printed in the United States of America

Library of Congress Cataloging-in-Publication Data

DiGiulio, Robert C., 1949–
    Educate, medicate, or litigate? What teachers, parents, and
administrators must do about student behavior / by Robert C. DiGiulio.
        p.   cm.
    Includes bibliographical references (p.   ) and index.
    ISBN 0-7619-7823-2 (cloth: alk. paper)
    ISBN 0-7619-7824-0 (pbk.: alk. paper)
    1. School violence—United States—Prevention.   2. Socialization—
United States.   I. Title.
    LB3013.3 .D53   2000
    371.7′82—dc21   00-012043

This book is printed on acid-free paper.

01   02   03   04   05   06   07   7   6   5   4   3   2   1

Acquisitions Editor:	Robb Clouse
Corwin Editorial Assistant:	Kylee Liegl
Production Editor:	Nevair Kabakian
Editorial Assistant:	Candice Crosetti
Typesetter/Designer:	Lynn Miyata
Cover Designer:	Tracy E. Miller

Contents

Preface

Our concern about poor behavior among young people goes back to ancient times. Certainly, there is nothing new about antisocial behavior or about societies' reactions to and disapproval of that behavior. Yet, although the concern is long-standing, today's circumstances are quite different from the past. Only in the last century have we seen the word *violence* used in connection with *youth,* and only in the last couple of decades have we seen *violence* connected to *schools.*

Indeed, this 21st century finds our societies quite challenged in several respects: Young people—indeed, all people—have greater access to weapons and access to the kinds of weapons that are capable of inflicting great harm. In addition, although all young people in the past were exclusively molded by the messages and models of those around them, messages today emanate from attractive media such as television, film, video, audio, and the Internet. In the past, society had relatively strong institutions to countervail or balance messages, including parents, extended family, religious organizations, and more recently, public and private educational institutions (schools). Each of these institutions has grown less influential over the latter part of the 20th century. Last and most subtle, today, a public disdain for socialization (it is too encumbering) appears to have arisen. We have a mixed view of the value of our educational institutions—in general, they're poor except for the schools in our community—and the role educators can and should play in addressing antisocial and violent behavior ("It's not my job to teach good behavior—that should be learned at home."). The widespread medicating of our youth is a relatively new measure ("He's off the walls because he didn't take his Ritalin."). Also new is the perception of student-as-suspect, an emphasis on legal measures taken against children, consisting mostly of school suspension and expulsion and of civil trial and incarceration (one-strike-and-you're-out or one-strike-and-you're-in, depending on whether it's school or prison). My concern with medical and legal measures in particular is that those responses to antisocial behavior among young people are generally reactive, after-the-fact measures. Despite the wide use of the word *preventive,* few contemporary measures actually prevent anything. Fewer and fewer measures, it seems, take best advantage of the potentially great socializing power and preventive strength of the schools and the community.

Ever since I began my teaching career in the inner-city public schools of New York City, I have realized how important a school and its staff are in the socialization process and how much of what is learned in school carries over, often quietly, into the home, neighborhood, and community. This value of the schools' role has increased, but there has not been a commensurate increase in the support that schools receive toward this end. Toward the goal of socialization of young people, schools work best with support not from remote governmental organizations or from in-your-face security measures but from the people within—from the schools' administrators, staff, and faculty. Support must also come from the people without, but not too far without—from the neighborhood, the local school board, and community businesses as well as from community religious and social organizations. In his prominent 1995 *Harvard Educational Review* article "Preventing and Producing Violence," professor Pedro A. Noguera summed up these ideas quite well:

> The urban schools that I know that feel safe to those who spend their time there don't have metal detectors or armed security guards, and their principals don't carry baseball bats. What these schools do have is a strong sense of community and collective responsibility. Such schools are seen by students as sacred territory, too special to be spoiled by crime and violence, and too important to risk one's being excluded. Such schools are few, but their existence serves as tangible proof that there are alternatives to chaotic schools plagued by violence. (p. 207)

Perhaps the greatest tragedy lies in the fact that when it comes to responding to and preventing antisocial and violent behavior, we know what works, what needs to be done; and we know how to do it. Research and practice have yielded clear and promising directions that schools have taken and can take with regard to student antisocial behavior. We are not stumbling in the dark, groping for a panacea, although it sometimes seems that way to the public, to parents, to the business community, and to educators. In relation to elucidation of the problem and possible solutions, my book has several goals. First, I wish to shed light on what has been called *the culture of violence,* including the culture of incivility that seems to be part of that larger phenomenon. I will then look at some of the most persistent myths that affect our perceptions of schools, myths that serve to disempower schools, particularly in their ability to address antisocial and violent behavior. Drawing on writings and research from other nations, I will then provide an overview of ways that young people throughout the world learn social behavior from their home, from peers, and from schools. Next, I will look closely at what factors contribute to the development of antisocial and violent behavior. Finally, I will draw together what research and practice say about best practices: what works when it comes to responding to antisocial behavior, with an emphasis on the best school-level preventive responses to antisocial behavior and the best community-level preventive responses. I have written this book for both the professional and the layman, for the student and practitioner, for the person who works in the schools each day and for informed taxpayers, concerned with the ways their tax dollars are being spent. Ultimately, I have written this book for all our children.

Acknowledgments

I have never worked with a finer publishing house than Corwin Press, a most caring and proficient organization. In particular, I am glad I worked with Acquisitions Editor Robb Clouse, Books Production Editors Nevair Kabakian and Denise Santoyo, Editorial Assistant Kylee Liegl, and Copy Editor Hawley Roddick. Their expertise greatly facilitated the publication of my book and helped turn a difficult task into a pleasing one.

Friends Pam Rush, Darlene Witte, Paul K. Robbins, Al Cannistraro, and Bruce Marlowe gave helpful advice about the manuscript, and my children, Angela and Matthew DiGiulio, provided encouragement and inspiration. My colleagues and students at Johnson State College have also given me much stimulation and insight, as have the many teachers whom I have interviewed and observed (and continue to interview and observe). The people at Project Harmony facilitated my visits and academic work in Finland and Russia, enabling me to broaden my perspective on international schooling and socialization. Dr. Herb Tilley, Provost of Berne University, has helped me add to my grasp of international education in the Western Hemisphere. In addition, I continue as a postdoctoral student at the University of South Africa in Pretoria, engaged in socioeducational research under the guidance of my promoter, Dr. Anne-Mari Dicker, and joint promoter, Dr. Erna Prinsloo. They have offered wise and kind suggestions toward my ongoing socioeducational research.

Finally, my wife and friend, Emily DiGiulio, helped me keep a perspective and a sense of humor throughout the writing of this book.

Corwin Press would like to acknowledge the following reviewers:

Gus Douvanis
University of West Georgia
Carrollton, GA

J. Jeffrey Grill
Athens State University
Athens, AL

Ian Harris
University of Wisconsin—
    Milwaukee
Milwaukee, WI

G. Roy Mayer
California State University,
    Los Angeles
Los Angeles, CA

Jonathan Plucker
Indiana University
Bloomington, IN

Johnny Purvis
University of Southern
    Mississippi
Hattiesburg, MS

Chester Quarles
University of Mississipi
Oxford, MS

Vincent Schiraldi
Justice Policy Institute
Washington, DC

About the Author

ROBERT C. DIGIULIO is Education Professor at Johnson State College in Vermont. He earned his PhD in human development and education from the University of Connecticut and his BA and MS in education from St. John's University. He began his teaching career in the New York City public school system, where he taught for a number of years. His 30-year career as an educator includes teaching at the elementary, middle, junior high, and college levels, with experience ranging from crowded urban schools to a one-room schoolhouse. He has also served as an elementary school principal, educational researcher, consultant, and writer.

As an educational consultant, he codeveloped Teen Test, a vocational counseling program for adolescents. He also coauthored educational computer software called Language Activities Courseware and authored its teacher's guide. His *Teacher* magazine article "The 'Guaranteed' Behavior Improvement Plan" was recognized as having one of the highest total readership scores of any of that magazine's articles.

He has authored numerous books including *When You Are a Single Parent, Effective Parenting, Beyond Widowhood,* and *After Loss,* selected by *Reader's Digest* as their featured condensed book in May 1994. He is a contributing author to *The Oxford Companion to Women's Writing in the United States* and *Marriage and Family in a Changing Society* and is the coauthor of *Straight Talk About Death and Dying.*

Most recently (1999), he has written "Nonviolent Interventions in Secondary Schools: Administrative Perspectives," a chapter in *Peacebuiliding for Adolescents: Strategies for Educators and Community Leaders,* edited by Ian M. Harris and Linda R. Forcey. Dr. DiGiulio's most recent book is *Positive Classroom Management: A Step-by-Step Guide to Successfully Running the Show Without Destroying Student Dignity.* Published by Corwin Press, its second edition was issued in 2000.

His interests include international education, child and adolescent behavior, and classroom management. Dr. DiGiulio's research interests lie in examining the roles of the parent, teacher, and school in child and adolescent socialization. Recently, he wrote a successful grant awarding a Fulbright Scholar-in-Residence to Johnson State College. He is a member of Project Harmony's Advisory Board on Education Programs and is presently studying with the Faculty of Education at the University of South Africa in Pretoria. He resides with his family in northern Vermont.

1

A Culture of Violence

Antisocial behavior of students in and around American schools has recently become a topic of serious concern throughout the nation. In its extreme form (violence), antisocial behavior has received notorious publicity due largely to tragic shootings at schools in modest American towns such as Jonesboro, Arkansas; Springfield, Oregon; Lake Worth, Florida; and Littleton, Colorado, where disturbed students killed other students, teachers, and in the latter case, themselves as well. When a first-grade student was shot to death in her Michigan classroom by a fellow student, a magazine wondered, "What should we do with a 6-year-old killer?" (Periscope, 2000, p. 6). These extreme cases of explosive violence are particularly frightening, for they arise suddenly, with little or no warning, yet with great force; these serious acts of violence are "like floods and tornadoes, not easy to predict or to prevent" (Toby, 1993/1994, p. 4).

Less extreme antisocial behaviors such as assaults, fighting, threats, and student misbehavior receive less publicity, yet they are much more common than murderous rampages. A newsmagazine reported that almost 1 in 4 students and 1 in 10 teachers say they have been victims of some form of serious antisocial behavior on or near school property (Welsh, 1999). Indeed, for many years, student antisocial behavior has been the most serious school-related concern of the American public; for each year since 1969, "lack of discipline" in school has ranked at or near the top in national surveys of the American public on the problems faced by American public schools (Rose & Gallup, 1999, p. 42). Educators have been concerned as well. Over 1,000 American teachers surveyed revealed their concern over in-school violence (Metropolitan Life Insurance Company, 1993, pp. 35-58), yet despite that concern, only 4% of all teachers rate the public schools in their own communities as not safe and orderly (Langdon & Vesper, 2000).

Violent behavior is not limited to schools and is not unique to America. Over 30 years ago, United Nations Secretary U Thant spoke of the widespread expression of violence in television, literature, and the film industry. He said that "violence seems to have been consecrated in many parts of the world" (Menninger, 1968, p. 158). Indeed, his pronouncement remains true today, for a review of recent literature reveals that antisocial behavior and violence are concerns in South Africa (Botha, 1995; Burnett, 1998; Hamber, 1998; Straker, 1996; van Eeden, 1996), Canada (MacDonald & da Costa, 1996), Australia (Fitzclarence, 1995), Germany (Niebel, 1994), Japan (Takahashi & Inoue, 1995), and in third-world and emerging nations as well as highly industrialized nations (Ohsako, 1997). (During teaching visits to urban and rural Russia in 1996 and 1998, I met teachers and administrators who told me that Russian schools faced problems similar to Western nations' schools; the only difference, one principal confided, was that "you keep better statistics!")

Perhaps to a greater extent than other industrialized nations, South Africa is undergoing a dramatic transformation, brought about by sweeping changes including the recent abolition of apartheid and the adoption of a new Constitution. Its society faces multiple challenges affecting the education of its young people, including rapid population growth, a shortage of funding for education, a multiplicity of racial and cultural linguistic mixes, and also a disintegrating family structure and a politicized educational system (Prinsloo, Vorster, & Sibaya, 1996). These factors are connected to a rapid rise in crime in other nations as well. Even Singapore, regarded as a stable nation strongly intolerant of disorder, has seen its arrest rate of young people more than double between 1991 and 1995 (Reuters, 1996).

Certainly, all violence is not the same. Some acts are utterly unexplainable and unpredictable, such as murders committed on impulse or shootings because someone snapped, as in the case of disgruntled employees, or those reacting violently to a seemingly mild rebuke. Unexplainable and unpredictable violence also includes serial killing or mass murder, and violence directed at babies or other innocents (such as victims of the Tylenol poisonings in the Chicago area). Some forms of violence may appear to be more easily explained, but they still remain difficult or impossible to predict or forestall. These include natural disasters such as floods, tornadoes, and earthquakes, and human disasters, including tragedies such as the murder-suicides at Columbine High School in 1999.

On the other hand, there are forms of violence—perhaps most forms of violence—that are both predictable and preventable, such as the violence that arises from antisocial behavior. This more serious form of antisocial behavior is learned from the social milieu—from a "culture of violence" (Tadesse, 1997, p. 2) that surrounds our young people and shapes their social and school experiences. This culture of violence is a form of social narrative, a "story or account of events, experiences or the like, whether true or fictitious" (Flexner, 1987, p. 1278) that is shared by a group, community, or nation. The main story line within the culture-of-violence narrative is that the world is a dangerous place and that one must be prepared (armed, usually, in some way) to respond strongly in order to survive. It is thus a self-fulfilling prophecy.

Educators Kauffman and Burbach (1997) examined the connection between the culture of violence and human behavior and found that a "social ecology" (p. 321) supports and nurtures antisocial behavior. This social ecology reinforces a sense of incivility: impoliteness and discourtesy directed toward others that serves as a basis for subsequent violence. The authors cited a recent survey by *U.S. News and World Report* that revealed 9 out of 10 Americans believe incivility to be a serious problem. Moreover, 91% believed that the decline in civility also contributes to violence. For example, fighting is the most common form of physical violence in high schools, and like other forms of violence, fighting usually begins as the result of a trigger mechanism—an act that sets the stage for and facilitates the onset of violent behavior. Although fighting has always had triggers (such as competition over turf or vying for a lover), Kauffman and Burbach (1997) claim that today the triggers are far more sensitive, involving "a quickness to bristle, an anticipation of offense. It's a tendency to have hurt feelings with no evidence of malicious intent on the part of someone else, a quickness to anger. . . . " This hair trigger is followed by a tendency to respond strongly to the real or perceived slight: "He dissed me, so I took him out." "She offended us, so she's not fit for public office" (p. 321).

Retribution is essentially the destructive crux of the culture-of-violence narrative. Those of us who have driven on an American highway have seen this phenomenon as "road rage," where a quick hair trigger is coupled with a strong response and usually in the most dangerous of situations.

A Culture of Antisocial Behavior

More accurately, then, we should speak of a broader "culture of antisocial behavior," which includes acts of extreme violence but also the less violent, everyday acts of incivility. (I will use the term *antisocial behavior* to encompass all degrees of interpersonal violence from rudeness to murder.) But why does it seem that there is more antisocial behavior today, and that incivility and retribution are part of our prevailing social narrative? On one hand, it appears that a sense of permission is secured from the culture to behave in antisocial ways and that social conditions are more favorable for expression of, and support for, antisocial behavior and that potential inhibitors of antisocial behavior are less potent. The preliminary evidence seems to support that idea: A 1998 survey by the Josephson Institute on Ethics (1999) of over 20,000 students revealed that 70% of all male high school students said they hit a person in the previous 12 months because they were angry. Female students were less likely to hit another person, yet 63% of high school girls said they hit someone in anger during the past year. When young adolescents are questioned after violent acts, they will usually reply that they felt justified in their actions. Their sense of retribution is powerful in these situations, with a compelling—and justified—need to "get back at" another who "had it coming."

There is a deceptive face to our attitudes: Despite the outward prohibitions against antisocial behavior in Western culture, yet perhaps as a result of those prohibitions, students who act antisocially *may be among the most popular of students.* Bullies, for example, are not necessarily unpopular. In fact, a recent study found they are often quite popular, reinforced and rewarded by both teachers and peers for their antisocial behavior (Rodkin, Farmer, Pearl, & Van Acker, 2000). In that study, one third of the most popular boys studied "were extremely antisocial, tending to argue, be disruptive, and start fights" (Lenihan, 2000, n.p.). Yet, these students can also be considered to be "cool" by some peers, and praised for being "assertive" by teachers (who may praise the student's nonbullying behavior in the hope of catching them being good, so to speak). Contrary to the common assumption that bullies are basically insecure individuals under a tough surface, empirical results point in the other direction: Bullies have little anxiety or insecurity and tend to be aggressive toward adults as well as peers (Olweus, 1995).

There is an interesting connection between these findings on bullies and other recent research that found that "bossier preschool kids are healthier" (Elias, 2000, p. 6). Pediatrician W. Thomas Boyce studied 69 middle-class, preschool students, and found that less aggressive children showed higher levels of stress than highly aggressive children. Children who were relatively timid, as well as those who were more likely to exhibit prosocial behavior, showed relatively higher stress reactions in school. These children seemed to function best in orderly, calm classrooms "where chaotic and unpredictable conditions don't require aggressive, outgoing behavior by youngsters" (p. 6). The most dominant children—who showed the lowest physical reaction to stress—also exhibited the worst acting-out behavior. The problem seemed to lie in the context of the classroom: The typical, contemporary preschool classroom may now be a place in which children who are most aggressive have less stress and children who act less aggressively are more stressed. Today's teachers may be inadvertently enabling strong behavior by being less inclined than in the past to respond strongly to aggressive student behavior (through physical restraint, punishment, and strong words), giving tacit permission for aggressive behavior. Teachers today may be more predisposed toward having students work it out for themselves rather than rely on teacher intervention, and that circumstance places the less aggressive child at increased risk.

Noam Chomsky (1994) states that aggression—and even the desire to kill—is innate, and "there are circumstances under which this aspect of our personality will dominate." He adds "that there are other circumstances in which other aspects will dominate. If you want to create a humane world, you change the circumstances" (p. 76). Circumstances surrounding young people often work to encourage antisocial behavior, and this too is part of the social narrative, which includes images of antisocial behavior by athletes, actors and actresses, and politicians. Closer to home, parents promote antisocial behavior not only when they abuse or neglect their children but also when they actively model and advocate in-your-face behavior. At a recent September Open House at a middle school in a fairly wealthy suburban Connecticut community, the new principal delivered an address to the gathered parents. She included in her opening remarks that she was immediately impressed by how strongly assertive students seemed to be at this school: "They get right in your face if they disagree with you," she said, "much more so than students did" at her previous school assignment in the Midwest (A. R. Vega, personal communication, September 18, 1999). Although the principal intended her observation to be one of several simple points of contrast between two schools, it was taken as a compliment by parents, several of whom nodded in agreement and some of whom applauded, no doubt pleased that their preadolescents were perceived to be standing up for themselves. (Had combative 1950s baseball manager Leo Durocher said, "Nice guys finish last," to this group of suburban Connecticut parents, they would have been in agreement.) In response to these aggressive parental attitudes, efforts are being made to rein in some parents whose zeal is excessive: Parents in Jupiter, Florida, are now required to enroll in a good-sportsmanship class before their children are permitted to play sports, and parents in Los Angeles must now sign a "promise of good (parental) behavior" form when their children play team sports (Fanning, 2000, p. 7). What were once unwritten, shared agreements and understandings of what acceptable public behavior is seem today to have evaporated.

Over 100 years ago, eminent sociologist Émile Durkheim offered an insightful perspective on what may be one underlying cause of our present culture of antisocial behavior. The prosperity that people in industrialized nations have enjoyed has altered their perceptions: The middle class has been convinced by its newly acquired wealth that it is itself quite powerful, and each individual is quite independent of others. Because wealth does open doors of opportunity and access, wealthy people come to believe that *all* doors, real and metaphorical, must open to them. When they do not, the reaction is quite strong: "I am angry; I have been cheated." Durkheim (1951) said it more succinctly:

> Lack of power, compelling moderation, accustoms men to it . . . Wealth, on the other hand, by the power it bestows, deceives us into believing that we depend on ourselves only. Reducing the resistance we encounter from objects, it suggests the possibility of unlimited success against them. The less limited one feels, the more intolerable all limitation appears. (p. 254)

In today's words, Durkheim is saying we have a diminished tolerance for frustration, resulting in a dangerous sense of entitlement. Antisocial and even violent behavior results from the frustration we experience when we see ourselves as being thwarted. When the car in front of us does not instantly move ahead on a green light or we find ourselves on a supermarket checkout line that moves slowly or not at all, we take this event personally and react strongly: Limitation and hindrance feel absolutely unbearable.

In later writings, Durkheim emphasized a hopeful alternative perspective on this darkening story of human behavior. In order for children to learn prosocial behavior, Durkheim (1961) said children must first be oriented toward the well-being of others; "Moral behavior demands an inclination toward collectivity" (p. 233). He emphasized that this *inclination* is not an automatic process; children will not on their own arrive at these understandings or acquire these inclinations. We can't completely let children fight their own battles or work it out for themselves, with little or no adult support and guidance, modeling, or leadership. Although he acknowledged the importance of family and home in the acquisition of prosocial behavior, Durkheim felt that teachers and schools were in a particularly advantageous position, because they could create a climate (social ecology) that would foster this inclination, even if children had not received prosocial teaching at home. Because teachers and schools represented the child's first contact with other, unrelated individuals, Durkheim (as well as his contemporaries Maria Montessori, Friedrich Froebel, and Rudolf Steiner) believed that school presented a society in microcosm, providing the child's first and most significant opportunity for socialization.

Instead of fostering an inclination toward collectivity, it appears that schools in America have not only deemphasized a prosocial orientation toward others, but in many situations, schools can also be seen to be fostering antisocial behavior. American culture has always emphasized the strongly independent individual. This emphasis on the individual has informed the dualistic way we regard the responsibility inherent in antisocial behavior and the consequences we prescribe: When there is failure, we look to identify the individual who is to blame, who is at fault, who is to suffer the consequences, to be made to pay. On the other hand, we compassionately make an exception from blame for those who are sick and thus not fully responsible for their behavior. Schools have followed both lines of reasoning in responding to antisocial behavior: If students' behavior is bad, but the individual is diagnosed as being sick, we medicate. If students' behavior is simply bad, absent any diagnosis of sickness, we punish them, typically with suspension, expulsion, and increasingly, incarceration.

To Medicate or to Litigate?

Particularly over the last three decades, the United States has seen a diminished emphasis on addressing antisocial behavior through educational approaches, while there have been increased emphases on addressing antisocial behavior through medicinal and criminal-justice approaches. There are many known, undesirable side effects in medicating children to treat their antisocial behavior, yet the trend toward medicating is particularly disturbing because it has lately and increasingly involved young and preschool-age children. A recent, widely circulated cartoon lampooned this development. It depicted a large dump truck backed up to an elementary schoolhouse, poised to make a delivery. The word *Ritalin* was printed on the truck's body, and in the cartoon's foreground was a street sign commonly seen in American suburban communities that provided the ironic punch line: The sign warned street drug dealers that this was a Drug-Free Schools Zone. Yet the problem is very serious: The number of U.S. children who have been placed on antidepressants and stimulants (drugs such as Ritalin and Prozac) has grown enormously over the past decade, and these drugs are now more likely than ever before to be administered to young children, including preschoolers (Zito et al., 2000). Study Director Julie Zito warned that the effects of these drugs on young children have not been assessed. Joseph Coyle of Harvard Medical School warned that administering psychotropic drugs to young children "could have deleterious effects on the developing brain." Perhaps most troubling is what he believes may be behind the push to medicate children. Medical assistance programs such as Medicaid (medical insurance for poor Americans) have lately "quite limited" their coverage for more thorough evaluation of behavioral disorders and have limited the patient to no more than one type of clinical evaluation per day. "Thus," Coyle concludes, "the multidisciplinary clinics of the past that brought together pediatric, psychiatric, behavioral and family dynamic expertise for difficult cases have largely ceased to exist." As a result, children with behavioral disturbances "are now increasingly subjected to quick and inexpensive pharmacologic fixes" (Reuters, 2000, n.p.).

In a comparison of pediatric visits to physicians between 1979 and 1996, medical researchers found that psychosocial problems (emotional and attentional disorders) increased from 6.8% to 18.7% of all visits (Kelleher, McInerny, Gardner, Childs, & Wasserman, 2000). Children with attention-deficit/hyperactivity disorder (ADHD) were far more likely to be identified in 1996 as compared with 1979, and they were more than twice as likely to be prescribed medications (32% of ADHD-diagnosed children in 1979 compared with 78% of ADHD-diagnosed children in 1996). The research team noted that these increases in psychosocial problems were associated with increases in the proportion of single-parent families as well as with Medicaid enrollment between 1979 and 1996.

Even more widespread than the emphasis on medicating children has been a growing reliance on reactive measures to youthful antisocial behavior, primarily litigation. These measures include the established criminal-justice progression of detection, apprehension, adjudication, and incarceration. Litigative approaches have gained favor lately in industrialized nations such as Great Britain, Australia, the United States, and South Africa, where the police-court-prison infrastructure has grown exponentially. For instance, in these nations, prisons are being built at a more rapid pace than ever before (in particular, maximum-security prisons). Private firms such as Corrections Corporation of America and Wackenhut Corrections Corporation have played a large part in this building surge. Recently, Wackenhut announced that "its South African consortium, South African Custodial Services (SACS), has signed a Project Development Agreement with the Government of South Africa for the design, construction, financing and operation of a 3,024-bed maximum security prison at Louis Trichardt, in South Africa's Northern Province" (Wackenhut Corrections Corporation, 1999, pp. 1-2). The same Wackenhut Corrections Corporation held a ribbon-cutting ceremony when it opened its new, 480-bed, maximum-security "youthful offender correctional facility" (prison) near Baldwin, Michigan. It began receiving inmates in July 1999. This facility is solely for boys aged 13 through 19, adolescents who have been sent to prison under new Michigan state laws mandating adult-type sentencing and prison terms for children and adolescents as young as 11, 12, and 13 years of age. Nationally, the number of children in this category more than doubled over a 12-year period: The U.S. Department of Justice reported that the number of young adolescents under the age of 18, who were convicted as adults, jumped from 3,400 in 1985 to 7,400 in 1997 (Johnson, 2000).

Even children who have not been charged with or convicted of a crime are at risk of being incarcerated, sent to what the U.S. Department of State calls "Behavior Modification Facilities," located outside the United States in Jamaica, Mexico, and Samoa. In a real-life scenario reminiscent of *Pinocchio*, where bad boys are sent to Pleasure Island to turn into donkeys with no hope of return, these facilities "isolate the children in relatively remote sites, restrict contact with the outside world and employ a system of graduated levels of earned privileges and punishments to stimulate behavior change." In these settings, children's "communications privileges" are limited. Parents typically sign a contract authorizing staff to act as agents for the parents and take whatever action may be necessary toward the "health, welfare, and progress" of the children (U.S. Department of State, 1999a, n.p.).

Certainly, there is a concern about violent behavior throughout the world, and although societies do need secure places to detain their most dangerous citizens, when a society's children and youths are considered to be among the most dangerous of its citizens, an ominous state of affairs exists. It is quite troubling when childhood is depicted within the social narrative as a period of deviant, antisocial behavior. Alexander Cockburn (1996) refers to this as a "war on kids," in which adult violence is "handed down in the form of blows, sexual predation and punishment" (p. 7). Aside from the damaging socialization that is being fostered by the emphasis on medicinal and adjudicative responses, it is also a question of resources: Many states' and nations' (and parents') financial resources are increasingly being channeled toward efforts that address the anticipation of violence and the aftereffects of violence (such as building new prisons and installing home security systems) instead of toward efforts to prevent those aftereffects from coming about and instead of efforts to address the root causes of violence. Perhaps worse is that these national and international adjudicative efforts are made at the macro level: the highest, governmental level of society. This is the level that is furthest from the individual (the micro level) and far from the level of the community and its institutions, such as schools (the meso level).

This recent and enlarged macro-level emphasis on reactive governmental responses has filtered down to the meso level, to the schools. In France, officials temporarily closed schools in northern cities recently in response to incidents of violence (Doland, 2000), and violence by Japanese public school children and adolescents in 1998 rose 24% over 1997 levels (Sakurai, 1999). Both nations have increased security and reporting measures in response. Researcher Toshio Ohsako (1997) has collected case studies of in-school violence in nations as diverse as Jordan, Ethiopia, Malaysia, Israel, Slovakia, and several Central American countries, noting how all are looking at ways to manage violence in and through their schools. In America, public schools have reacted to political pressure to take action by visible measures, such as increasing their use of metal detectors, video cameras, and trained dogs, and expanding their hiring of security guards and police officers. Many American school districts are now spending hundreds of thousands of dollars annually for these security measures, often paying for them out of school funds originally earmarked for instruction and educational programs for students (Jones, 1999). However, the most common and widespread reaction to antisocial behavior by students—and the response most favored by U.S. high school administrators—is removing students from school through suspension and expulsion (Astor, Meyer, & Behre, 1999). These measures are popular despite the fact that there is no evidence that they reduce antisocial and violent behavior by students (Skiba & Peterson, 1999a). Furthermore, there is evidence that forceful, prison-like reactions such as strip searches of students and the use of dogs in school searches may worsen antisocial behaviors and create emotional harm in students (Hyman & Perone, 1998). Much research clearly shows that criminal-justice responses and environments that emphasize punitive measures serve to foster aggression, violent behavior, and vandalism (Azrin, Hake, Holz, & Hutchinson, 1965; Berkowitz, 1983; Hutchinson, 1977; Mayer, 1995). Even medical researchers have concluded that America's predominant response to violence has been a reactive one—to pour resources into deterring and incapacitating violent offenders by apprehending, arresting, adjudicating, and incarcerating them through the criminal-justice system. This approach, however, has not made an appreciable difference (Mercy, Rosenberg, Powell, Broome, & Roper, 1993, p. 11).

Schools: The Problem or the Solution?

The rise in medication and litigation is particularly incongruous, ascending at a time when we have learned much of the nature and circumstances of antisocial behavior as well as the results of increased research attention on how to best prevent its development. Anthony Biglan (1995) of the Oregon Research Institute emphasized that it is indeed

> ironic that we have such high rates of serious antisocial behavior at the same time that the behavioral sciences are making so much progress in understanding and intervening on the contextual conditions that contribute to the development of antisocial behavior. (p. 479)

Indeed, the past 25 years have seen a rich amount of high-quality research into effective and best practices in addressing student behavior and antisocial behavior. These include a variety of global measures, such as curricular reform, conflict resolution, violence prevention programs, peace education, and restructuring the school to more closely resemble a community. Although the effectiveness of some measures (such as certain types of violence-prevention programs) has not been proved, schools are showing themselves in many ways to be not the problem but part of the solution. There are ways that schools are following Durkheim's advice by orienting and inclining children toward prosocial behavior.

For one example, we know that the context of the classroom and school is a crucial variable that influences levels of violence—and crime—within schools. One way to improve that context has been to reduce its scale within. This is being done in many large middle schools in the United States. Schools have begun to divide huge blocks of classrooms into smaller units called *houses*—schools in microcosm—that provide a better level of closeness, decrease alienation, and thus foster a sense of community. Schools are also orienting students toward prosocial behavior through peacemaking strategies and peace-building approaches. Peacemaking includes teaching students to resolve disputes without violence, typically through peer mediation and positive communication, whereas peace building "sees the problem of school violence as a reflection of a violent culture" (Harris, 2000, p. 7), helping students choose ways to change the culture, as well as keep themselves safe.

As a second example, much promise seems to lie at the micro level of teacher-to-student relationships. There we have discovered (actually, rediscovered) the value of teacher interventions: the enormous benefit for students when teachers do not turn their backs on antisocial behavior. Recent research has established the importance of the teacher's use of teachable moments within the classroom as promoters of positive student socialization. We have only recently learned that there is an important connection between time and place with regard to student antisocial behavior: All behavior takes place in context, and some locations in schools and times during the day are more likely to be settings for antisocial behavior than others (Astor et al., 1999). The authors' socioenvironmental and transactional perspectives on in-school violence provide a holistic landscape of antisocial and violent behavior in schools. These perspectives lend support to the idea that serious antisocial behaviors—and the places and times where and when those behaviors occur—are interrelated, as are student antisocial behaviors and the way teachers respond to—or ignore—those behaviors. In essence, we have rediscovered that person-to-person relationships are extremely powerful in preventing antisocial behavior, through both the teacher's active interventions into student behaviors and the teacher's modeling of prosocial behaviors and mutual respect (Tierno, 1996). We are learning that it is the way Ms. Jackson teaches within her classroom and how she does not turn her back on students in the hallway that make a school feel safe.

A third illustration that points to the way schools can be an essential part of the solution is provided by University of California researcher Pedro Noguera (1995), who described a novel approach to modifying a school's context. He studied an inner-city junior high school in California that hired a local grandmother (instead of a security guard) to monitor students in school. "Instead of using physical intimidation to carry out her duties, this woman greets children with hugs." When the hugs prove to be insufficient to maintain prosocial behavior, "she admonishes them to behave themselves, saying she expects better from them" (p. 206). Many might laugh at the idea of hiring a grandmother instead of an armed guard, yet this school was the only school in its district in which no weapons were confiscated from students during that school year.

Summary

Educational measures take time, unlike medical and criminal-justice measures that appear to give immediate results (that these results do not solve any problems is rarely conceded, however). Educational measures are not quick fixes, but neither are they, of necessity, expensive. Perhaps what is most disturbing is how poorly publicized these three positive examples are. On the other hand, bad news seems to travel quite rapidly: Until it was exposed as a hoax, a list of how times have changed was widely circulated, showing how teachers in 1940 rated the top disciplinary problems as talking in class and chewing gum, whereas teachers of 1990 claimed their top disciplinary problems included teenage pregnancy, rape, and alcohol abuse. Investigations revealed the lists to be a hoax contrived by a man who simply compared his school experiences of 1940 with what he read in the newspapers and saw on television today (Bracey, 1994; O'Neill, 1994). His list was cited by magazine, Internet, and newspaper writers and columnists in the 1990s, including George Will, among many others. Misinformation that is conveyed, perpetuated, and compounded spreads like a computer virus, and is durable: 6 years after the how-times-have-changed hoax list was exposed by Bracey and others, Web sites such as the Troubled Teens Network (www.troubledteens.net/) continue to cite the 1940-versus-1990 "Public School Teachers Rate the Top Disciplinary Problems" lists as if they were factual. This misinformation phenomenon is of a type that is particularly damaging to schools, not only due to its durability but also because it is difficult for schools as a whole to rebut such allegations, having no generally accepted spokesperson or clearinghouse for accurate information. As a result, the public is encouraged to conclude that public schools are not only dangerous places but are also sources of violence in our society. Enemies of public education—including some politicians, educators, and religious leaders—are quick to capitalize on any bad news about schools. Bad news about schools, unfortunately, is a self-fulfilling prophecy: Educator Mari M. McLean (1995) points out that

> when an institution is seen as a violent place, those both inside and outside the institution will act and react to everything that happens within that frame of reference . . . (as a result), containing potential violence demands strict discipline, unquestioning obedience to authority, and mindless conformity. (p. 21)

Hence, schools become transformed by media myths, and the public is portrayed as clamoring for greater levels of control, punishment, and medication of young people. Focus is thus moved from academic achievement, and educational efforts to teach students prosocial behavior seem almost whimsical. Perhaps the most damaging outcome produced by the myths and falsehoods surrounding violence and the schools is that, in McLean's words, "When students view schools as prisons and teachers and administrators as guards and wardens, they will begin to behave more like prisoners than like students, and violence in the schools will become its own self-fulfilling prophecy."

This prevents schools from carrying out what should be their most vital role and saps what should be their greatest strength. Coincidentally, it also blunts what the public wants most from its schools: effective socialization of young people. In advocating for "building a gentler school," educators Vicky Dill and Martin Haberman (1995) say that schools are pivotal in providing options to violent behaviors and instilling prosocial student behavior. "Schools that forego this opportunity waste what may be the only chance to help many students succeed productively in society and avoid a life of crime. For students in poverty especially, school may be their only out" (p. 71). Schools may be our society's "only way out of" our culture of antisocial behavior as well.

Earlier, I asked if schools are the problem or the solution. On the one hand, schools are seen as the problem: We live in a society that appears to have grown either skeptical of or impatient with (or both) its schools. On the other hand, my argument is that schools have a fundamental and essential role to play in socializing young persons and in turning around our culture of antisocial behavior. Accordingly, throughout this work, I have used the terms *school violence* and *student violence* very carefully, not automatically as synonyms for *violence.* The difference is important. A review of recent works on the subject shows there to be an unfortunate tendency to routinely and easily connect *violence* with *school.* There is violence in school, but it is far more common within our homes, communities, neighborhoods, and within our society outside of school. Although I cannot deny there are instances of violent behavior by students (which I will look at in depth in Chapters 3 and 4), it is also true that schools remain safe places, and they remain the best places for our young to learn in-school prosocial behavior that can be carried outside school as civil behavior. Toward that end, my goals for this book are four: First, to look at the myths that surround the depiction of our schools as dangerous, violent places and to highlight some facts and realities of those places. Second, to shed light on the question of how we as humans learn social behavior. My third goal is to analyze and explore ways in which social behavior becomes antisocial and violent behavior. Fourth and last, my goal is to assemble and present the ways that our schools can best respond to antisocial behavior, in non-punitive, mostly preventive ways. These best practices have been drawn from the professional literature as well as from the experiences of many successful educators of children and adolescents in rural, suburban, and urban schools whom I have interviewed and whose work I have observed. In the following chapter, I will seek to shed light on the problem through a discussion of the myths and realities surrounding violent and antisocial behavior, particularly how those myths apply—and do not apply—to schools.

Myths and Realities
Schools, Violence, and Antisocial Behavior

Sometimes, things seem too good to be true. In 1971, a great deal of interest was generated by the news that an unusually gentle, thoroughly peaceful tribe was discovered living in caves deep in the forests of Mindanao, in the Philippines. Called *Tasaday,* they spoke an ancient tongue, and were so gentle that they had no words for *war* and no words for acts of aggression. Shortly after the fall of President Ferdinand Marcos, however, the Tasaday story was revealed to be an elaborate hoax. In 1989, Swiss anthropological researchers entered the area only to find that the caves reported to have been occupied by the Tasaday were empty, with no sign that any humans ever inhabited the area. Further inquiry revealed that officials interested in limiting tree cutting on forestland in the region of the South Cotabato Mountains in southern Mindanao contrived the Tasaday revelation. The hoax is perhaps most interesting because of the previously unknown degree of gentleness that the tribe allegedly possessed. These native Tasaday people "displayed no aggressive tendencies whatsoever, either to outsiders or to one another" (Wallechinsky & Wallace, 1975, p. 476) and had no weapons for hunting or war. Although they were not sociable in the sense of mixing with others, the Tasaday people's behavior was decidedly prosocial,

17

highly considerate of other members of their tribe, and even more unusual, they directed no aggressive behavior toward others not of their tribe.

Because we take so much for granted, in a worldwide culture of violence, such groups of peaceful humans would simply *have* to have been contrived, as they had been. Yet like all great mythology, this myth of the peaceful Tasaday reflected and pointed to truths about our human existence. For instance, it is true that many peaceful human groups have survived under difficult conditions since the Stone Age—groups in which individual behavior is oriented toward the benefit of others. The Netsilik of northern Canada, for example, have survived for centuries with no formal legal system and no formal systems for punishment, retribution, or rehabilitation. Instead, the Netsilik have relied on three central, unwritten codes of conduct: collaboration, in which they work together in hunting, preparing, and sharing food; kinship, the maintenance of a network of ties to nuclear and extended family; and patterning relationships, the forming of partnerships with unrelated others (Balikci, 1970, chaps. 3-6). Antisocial behavior is rare, minimized by the natural consequence of being excluded from the larger group in one of the most hostile climates on earth. But the Netsilik are not completely unusual, for prosocial behavior guided by unwritten codes of conduct exists in all human societies. This feature, however, has grown relatively weak in American society. Indeed, the word *prosocial* isn't to be found in any American or English dictionary or in any thesaurus. We have no English word, either, to denote an alternative to a formal legal system (except for negative terms such as *anarchy* or *chaos*).

Because contemporary American culture does not emphasize or prize prosocial behavior, it readily accepts many myths concerning antisocial behavior and violence, particularly as they pertain to young persons. Although the reasons for this situation are complex, it is clear that many myths are connected to our schools and the education system. It is only natural that schools have been drawn into the myths, because we have asked our schools to take on responsibility to cure society's ills. What role schools should play in addressing antisocial behavior and violence is unclear. Although the public supports socialization of students, there is little clear or deep understanding of the extent of violence in our society other than reports of crime in schools and schools that are violent. Although many teachers, students, and parents report they feel victimized by violence in some form, "a solid understanding of how much violence occurs in schools, and what that violence looks like, is lacking" (Greene, 1999, p. 58).

Indeed, the misunderstandings surrounding violence extend to the idea that schools are themselves sources and perpetuators of violent and antisocial behavior. Much of the perceptions and misperceptions about schools and antisocial behavior have been conveyed and perpetuated by and through the media. According to the Justice Policy Institute of the Children's Law Center, "Americans don't know what they know about youth violence from personal experience, they know what they know about youth violence from the media" (Brooks, Schiraldi, & Ziedenberg, 2000, n.p.). In the media, *youth violence* is often used interchangeably with *school violence.* I would like to first discuss in general media myths about schools and violence and then explore 10 persistent myths about schools and violence.

Media Myths About Schools and Violence

Since the earliest moving pictures were produced, teachers and students have been portrayed as caricatures, ranging from matronly teachers and silly, truant pranksters to the more modern demagogues and student murderers. In few cases have the portrayals of students or teachers been complimentary. One high school educator stated that "the entertainment industry's portrayal of public schools . . . has been anything but flattering" (McLean, 1995, p. 20). Especially over the past 50 years, films have generally portrayed schools as dysfunctional places of antisocial behavior and more recently, as places of serious violence.

One of the first serious films connecting violence with schools was the 1955 movie *Blackboard Jungle,* in which students subject a newly hired teacher and his family to intimidation. (The first weapon of simulated student-to-teacher violence was probably the switchblade knife snapped open and directed at teacher Glenn Ford in that film.) Previously, student-teacher relationships were benign, with students portrayed as docile and putty-like, easily shaped by the teacher's mere presence or stern glance. (Miss Crabtree of the 1930s Little Rascals film *Teacher's Pet,* and Wally Cox's *Mr. Peepers,* a 1950s TV situation comedy, come to mind.) In literature, Golding's *Lord of the Flies* was published about the same time as *Blackboard Jungle,* and it portrayed child-to-child antisocial behavior in chilling detail, behavior that, in the absence of adult authority, reached the highest level of violence (killing). Previously, 19th-century British fiction was filled with schoolboy-to-schoolboy antisocial behavior, but it was antisocial behavior rarely revealed to or directed at adults or society, and never was it of a highly violent nature.

Prior to the 1950s, the depiction in film of school-related antisocial behavior was mild; in many movies, it was completely nonexistent (*Goodbye, Mr. Chips*) or it was playful, consisting of pranks or truancy; playing hooky had delightful connotations in Little Rascals and Andy Hardy films, among others. Yet since *Blackboard Jungle*, films have tended to depict school-related antisocial behavior as violent behavior. *To Sir, With Love* (1967) portrayed tough British youths intimidating a new teacher, and *If . . .* (1968) showed violence at a private boys' prep school. The first one third of the 1989 film *Lean on Me* can be considered nonstop student violence, as pandemonium reigns until the bullhorn-and-baseball-bat-wielding principal, Joe Clark, single-handedly expels the disruptive students from his school. *Dangerous Minds* (1995) portrays an ex-U.S. marine who is challenged by her classroom filled with inner-city students. Their antisocial behavior—prominently tinged with sexual innuendo—is directed at her and at other students. In the end, the teacher wins by being more indestructible than the students (after all, she does know karate). A more authentic portrayal is found in *Stand and Deliver* (1987), based on the true story of high school mathematics teacher Jaime Escalante. His devotion to teaching—and hard work—help most of his inner-city Los Angeles students pass college-level, advanced-placement exams. But even here, the teacher confronts a dramatically hostile, highly threatening, and strongly antisocial group of students—modern-day versions of students in *Blackboard Jungle* in their gang affiliation and orientation toward intimidating the teacher. The Internet Movie Database (2000, n.p.) gives plot outlines for two versions of the film *Teacher's Pet*, filmed 70 years apart, that provide an interesting comparison: The plot outline of the first, a Little Rascals film released in 1930, states: "Jackie prepares a series of elaborate jokes for his new teacher" (us.imdb.com/Title?0021456). The plot outline of the most recent *Teacher's Pet*, released in 2000, reads: "A college coed falls for her teacher and will kill anyone who gets in her way" (us.imdb.com/Title?0217086).

In addition to the entertainment media promoting school-violence images, the news media have also contributed to the connecting of violence to schools. This has come about through sensationalizing news stories, and also by the presenting of news in a decontextualized fashion.

Given the short amount of time that can be dedicated to each story, news becomes a series of trivia bits, of sound bites. This precludes deep or critical thinking and prevents a careful analysis of information received. When the background of a story and extenuating circumstances (that might serve to dampen the story's novelty or shock value) are left out, viewers are left uninformed and, at times, misinformed. When television newscasters, for example, report on violence that has occurred in a school, rarely will they add that such violence is exceedingly rare. Instead, we hear phrases such as "another in a series of school shootings" and "what is becoming a familiar scenario in our nation's schools." Because most Americans get most of their information from television (Dorfman, Woodruff, Chavez, & Wallack, 1997), sensationalizing and decontextualizing have a profound impact on viewers' attitudes. Researchers at the Justice Policy Institute maintain that "the media has been a very poor teacher" when it comes to educating Americans on the important issues (Brooks et al., 2000, n.p.).

Perhaps the media messages have become stronger, more foreboding and inflammatory, because Americans have been exposed to and thus tolerant of higher and higher levels of violence. Americans may have grown numb to violence, with an arousal threshold that is quite high, causing media to crank up the intensity. Former New York Senator Daniel Moynihan offers this perspective on antisocial behavior. In his noted article *Defining Deviancy Down,* Moynihan (1993/1994) writes that what was in the past considered to be serious antisocial behavior has gradually been redefined and has become more likely to be accepted as normal behavior today. He offers examples, such as the St. Valentine's Day Massacre, in which four gunmen in Chicago shot seven gangsters on February 14, 1929. "The nation was shocked," he wrote. "The event became a legend. It merits not one but two entries in the *World Book Encyclopedia.*" Moynihan also points out that Los Angeles has the equivalent of a St. Valentine's Day Massacre several times a year, but because of a high level of exposure to and tolerance for higher and higher levels of violent behavior, each slaughter today "produces only moderate responses" (p. 16).

Violence at low or high levels touches on people's basic fear of death and is titillating, resulting in a covert fascination with death and with danger. English anthropologist Geoffrey Gorer (1965) aptly described this in his article title: "The Pornography of Death" (p. 192). Death is repulsive and repellent yet makes violence—the threat of death—captivating at some primal level. If we walk by a roped-off police investigation or auto accident site, we don't want to look, yet we look. This pornography of death surrounding real and potential violence has provided the entertainment industry with much profit. Violence, in combination with retribution, is an ancient theme, a theme highlighted in thousands of American films, from John Wayne's *Red River* to Charles Bronson's *Death Wish* to Mel Gibson's *Payback*. Recently, a new angle on this theme has emerged: Although the child alone who must fend for himself or herself in an uncaring world has historically been a popular theme, only recently have these children and adolescents taken matters into their own hands and truly fended for themselves in a world that has gone from uncaring to outright dangerous. For example, the movie *Home Alone* and its sequels come to mind, portraying Kevin, an American child whose parents and siblings fly to France, only to discover that he has been left behind. However, the child certainly needs no adult help in protecting himself from two adult intruders who suffer multiple indignities and injury from Kevin's guerrilla-warfare tactics. In the film *Man of the House,* bullies lock a student in a school locker, and no teachers or adults are around to intervene or let him out (the same situation occurs in *Lean on Me*). In each case of child-alone, children's antisocial behavior is justified: anger at parents or peers who are abusive, or anger directed at parents who divorce or who have taken on a new lover or spouse, or anger directed at otherwise innocent parents who simply are not with-it.

The entertainment value of child-alone notwithstanding, the child truly alone in the world is a real and increasingly serious problem, particularly in the third world and the developing world, and in impoverished communities in wealthy nations. Even more destructive than child abuse or neglect, the epidemic of AIDS is leaving many children with no parent. It is estimated that 28 million children will be orphaned in the next 10 years, mainly as a result of AIDS. In the report *Children on the Brink 2000,* co-author John Williamson warned that "the potential for social unrest, (and) social instability is pretty significant" ("AIDS Is Leaving a Generation of Orphans," 2000, p. 16). These children are the very ones who need the benefits of school for nutrition, safety, socialization, and academic reasons, yet these children are the least likely to have access to school. If the news and entertainment media wish to repay society for the benefits they have accrued from portraying children alone against a hostile world, the time has certainly come for the media to raise awareness of the plight of millions of the world's poorest children.

Although the battle against AIDS must take place on many fronts (medical, legal, and economic), it also must take place on an educational and social front. However, the potentially enormous contribution to be made by schools to the AIDS crisis or to the crisis of incivility cannot be realized in a climate of misinformation about the true relationship between schools and violence. We cannot say that "schools are dangerous and violent places" and in the same breath, say—and believe—that "schools hold the key to addressing serious social problems." As a first step toward resolving this dilemma, I would like to address myths about schools and violence, myths that are particularly pernicious, standing in the way of realizing the great potential schools hold for improving the lives of millions throughout the world.

Ten Persistent Myths About Schools and Violence

Myth #1: Schools Are Violent, Unsafe Places

Reality. Contrary to the image of schools as violent places, schools have traditionally been—and remain—*the safest of places in the world* for children and adolescents. Schools are also among the safest of workplaces for adults who are employed in them. In comparable years (1992 and 1993), a total of 76 students were murdered or committed suicide at school—an average of about 38 each year. (*At school* includes in school, on school property, on the way to or from school, and while attending or traveling to or from school-sponsored events.) Six years later, a total of 69 students suffered school-associated, violent deaths (murder and suicide) in a 2-year period. The number also decreased 40% from 1998 to 1999, from 43 to 26 (Brooks et al., 2000).

However, an even more dramatic (and relevant) comparison is found by examining the rate of murder outside school compared with the rate in school. Even looking at the years 1992-1993, when the number of in-school, violent deaths was highest for any 2-year period, young persons between the ages of 5 and 19 were *over 100 times more likely* to be murdered away from school than at school according to a report from the Office of Juvenile Justice and Delinquency Prevention (Snyder & Sickmund, 1999). In other years, out-of-school, violent deaths outnumber in-school, violent deaths several hundredfold. By any measure, schools are safe havens from serious violence, particularly in neighborhoods that are relatively dangerous.

In America, the frequency of violence in schools is related to school size and location. According to principals' reports, large schools (1,000 or more students) experience more than 3 times the incidence of violent behavior than small- and medium-sized schools (U.S. Department of Education, 1998). Violence is more likely to be reported in urban schools, compared with suburban and rural schools, although that difference has recently gotten smaller.

But perhaps the single most telling piece of evidence of the relative safety of schools comes from the insurance industry, experts in risk assessment. For kindergarten and Grades 1 to 12, student health insurance for bodily injury only, for the 2000-2001 school year, costs $16 for the Schooltime-Only Plan (covering bodily injury "while attending school when school is in session"). The Around-the-Clock Plan (covering bodily injury "at home, school or away . . . or just playing in the neighborhood") costs $62 per school year (Commercial Travelers Mutual Insurance Company, 2000, n.p.). Subtracting 7 hours for sleeping and subtracting $16 for the 7 hours of school, this latter coverage costs $46 for the 10-hour, nonschool period or $4.60 per hour for out-of-school coverage, compared with $2.28 per hour for in-school-only coverage. In other words, judging by the cost of insurance, the risk of bodily injury is more than twice as high out of school as in school.

Myth #2: School Violence Is Increasing

Reality. It is declining. Data from the Youth Risk Behavior Surveys were analyzed as to the numbers of students in high school grades who engaged in violent behaviors. In almost every category, the number of violent behaviors has decreased. In the period between 1991 and 1997, students involved in a physical fight decreased 14% from 42.5 to 36.6, the percentage of students injured in a fight decreased 20%, and the percentage of students who carried a weapon decreased by 30%. The researchers found each of these decreases to be statistically significant. They concluded by stating that these school-related declines between 1991 and 1997 parallel declines in homicide, nonfatal victimization, and other school crime rates (Brener, Simon, Krug, & Lowry, 1999).

Paradoxically, the American public believes that school violence is rising. Telephone polls conducted for *The Wall Street Journal* and for *NBC News* revealed that 71% of Americans surveyed thought a school shooting was likely to happen in their community, and 60% of those polled 7 months after the Columbine High School tragedy were worried a great deal about school violence. Interestingly, "polls showed that rural parents were most fearful of school violence, even though the overwhelming majority of serious crime against or by youth occurs in cities" (Brooks et al., 2000, n.p.).

Although the number of incidents of in-school violence is decreasing, the number of students suspended and expelled from schools has risen dramatically, almost doubling between 1974, when approximately 1.7 million students were suspended, and 1997, when 3.1 million students were suspended. Perhaps even more surprising is the reason for most school suspensions: They are for nonviolent causes, led by truancy, then tardiness. Fighting is third, followed by noncompliance with school policies. Similar to patterns seen in imprisonment rates, school suspensions fall disproportionately on male students and, in particular, on black male students, who are suspended at more than twice the rate of white students nationally, according to Norma Cantu, Assistant Secretary of Education for Civil Rights (Brooks et al., 2000).

Although the school violence statistics show a decreasing rate, statistics do not give a complete picture of antisocial behavior in schools. Over the past 30 years, the amount of incivility and lower-level, serious antisocial behavior has probably increased, and according to some educators and observers, increased dramatically. Anecdotal reports from teachers, administrators, and others who work with children and adolescents describe an increase in rudeness and harsh interpersonal behavior including "dissing," vulgar language, and what a teacher friend of mine refers to as "name-calling, eye-rolling, in-your-face behavior" directed at peers and adults. Incivility is more difficult to measure than violent crime: It's simple to count the number of arrests, injuries, and deaths but tough to quantify a climate of incivility. But as a guess, I would point to the dramatically increased number of school suspensions (which are mostly for nonviolent offenses) as a sign of the increase in incivility: Students with a negative or hostile attitude are probably more likely to be suspended than cooperative, prosocial students. It may, therefore, follow that principals are given just the grounds they need to suspend a student when the hostile student is truant or tardy or becomes involved in a fight.

Myth #3: Americans Are No More or Less Violent Than Anyone Else

Reality. Although schools are not the usual sites of violence or homicide in America, America does have a high rate of homicide compared with the rest of the world. U.S. children are 5 times more likely to be murdered than children in other industrialized countries. According to the Centers for Disease Control and Prevention, the United States had the highest rates of childhood homicide, suicide, and firearm-related deaths of 26 countries they studied. The greatest discrepancy between the United States and other industrialized nations, however, was in the proportion of firearm-related deaths of young persons, with the U.S. rates 12 times higher than rates in other industrialized nations. But even if we were to exclude firearm-related homicides, the remaining number of homicides of American children is almost 4 times other countries' rates (Reuters, 1997). Nonetheless, the vast majority of these homicides do not occur in school, at school-sponsored events, or on school property. Child homicides in the United States occur almost exclusively outside of and away from school.

Returning to the question of crime in America, it must be emphasized that most crime in America is nonviolent. Only 1 of every 10 persons arrested in the United States is arrested for a violent crime, and only 3% of all arrests are for a crime that has resulted in some form of bodily injury (Ambrosio & Schiraldi, 2000). The prison-school parallel is worthy of note: The vast majority of prisoners are serving prison time for nonviolent offenses, and the vast majority of suspended and expelled students have been put out of school due mostly to nonviolent offenses of truancy and tardiness. (Recently, the city of Detroit has melded the two penalties: Parents have been sent to prison when their children have been truant from school.)

Is America more violent than other nations? If the percentage of imprisoned people is the measure, then yes, Americans are more violent. But given the many paths to prison in America, violence is hard to pin down outside of crime and homicide figures, which themselves should be seen with caution, for crimes and homicides are defined differently in other nations. Violence may not come to the attention of reporting agencies in other nations as efficiently as it does in America and in American schools.

Myth #4: Young People Are Becoming More Violent

Reality. Although the U.S. rates of juvenile crime are high compared with other industrialized nations, those rates for violent crimes are falling.

Data from the FBI's *Uniform Crime Reports* (U.S. Department of Justice, 1993, 1998) show a 56% decline in juvenile homicide from 1993 to 1998, with a 30% decline in the overall rate of juvenile crime. The American Medical Association recently reported an analysis of data from 1991–1997 Youth Risk Behavior Surveys, which revealed that between 1991 and 1997, U.S. high school students became less likely to carry weapons, to engage in physical fights, and to be injured in physical fights (Brener et al., 1999).

This is a very surprising piece of information, given the fact that, first, almost all young children's homicides are gun related, and second, the estimated number of guns available to adolescents is perceived to have grown exponentially since the 1960s. In fact, the overall rate of adult and juvenile crime has been falling. In 2000, the FBI revealed that both violent crimes and property crimes had decreased nationwide by 7%, representing the eighth consecutive year that reported crime had fallen (Vicini, 2000). Yet the answer to the question "Are young people becoming more violent?" winds up hinging on how we define *young people,* for although juvenile crime rates (crimes committed by youths under 18 years of age) are falling, the crime rate of young male adults (those 18 years to 30 years of age) has risen fairly sharply.

Myth #5: Younger Children Are Committing More Murders

Reality. The murder rate has fallen. More precisely, the arrest rate of children has decreased: The rate of children younger than 13 years of age arrested for murder fell from .20 per million in 1964 to .11 per million in 1998 (22 children under the age of 13 were arrested for murder in 1998). Over that same 34-year period, the number of youths younger than 18 years of age arrested for any juvenile crime dropped by 30%, with rates for rape falling 29%, robbery decreasing 47%, and aggravated assault falling 27% (U.S. Department of Justice, 1993, 1998). However, there is no clear answer to this question, because there are variables, such as changes in the way children are charged (murder, homicide, involuntary manslaughter, etc.) and changes in the legal resources available between 1964 and 1998 (for example, the number of lawyers in America has risen significantly in that period). Thus we cannot conclude that younger and younger children are more likely—or less likely—to kill today than in years past. We simply don't know.

Myth #6: Older Students Are More Likely to Be Victims Than Younger Students

Reality. Young adolescents are more frequently victims of violence than older adolescents or younger children. Although schools are safe places, when they are unsafe, they are unsafe mostly for young adolescents. There is an uptick in the rates of violence around ages 11, 12, and 13. Violent victimization appears to peak at age 12, which is a time of physical transition (puberty) as well as educational transition (moving on to middle school). In both 1989 and 1995, students at age 12 were about 3 times more likely to be victims of violence than students at age 17 and 18. This is due in part, of course, to the fact that students who drop out of school tend to do so after age 16; those 17- and 18-year-olds who remain in school are generally not predisposed toward violent behavior. On the other hand, those age 16 and older who drop out are significantly more likely to be involved in a physical fight and carry a weapon. Adolescents who are not enrolled in school are also much more likely to smoke cigarettes and to use alcohol or other illegal drugs (Centers for Disease Control and Prevention, 1994). The value of school as a safe place is shown quite dramatically by such statistics.

Myth #7: The Only Effective Way to Stop Violence Is Through Punitive Measures

Reality. This is a persistent and dangerous myth that breeds much violence in itself. There is no evidence that harsh measures, such as suspension, expulsion, and incarceration, have any long-term and immediate effect on reducing antisocial or violent behavior in either in-school or non-school-related populations. Of course, expulsion, suspension, or incarceration brings relief to a school or classroom in which the offenders are removed. However, such measures simply relocate the problem: to the streets, to the mall, to the community, to the prisons. Police organizations do not tend to support zero-tolerance measures, for they know quite well where suspended and expelled students go and what they do when they are banned from school. Once a student has been put out of school, that student will be at a significantly higher risk for arrest, drug and alcohol use, and ultimately, premature death. Unfortunately, the political system cannot or will not take a look at the big picture involved with suspensions and expulsions, and this denial is worsening: Florida governor Jeb Bush signed into law a bill that exempted Florida schools from having the number of students suspended or expelled included in their school-accountability measures. Starting July 1, 2000, Florida schools could move toward their "excellence bonuses," as they were freed to suspend and expel as many students as they wished without accountability and without "fear their statewide grade might go down" (New Florida Laws, 2000, n.p.).

This does not mean that students with behavior disorders or violent students, in Florida or anywhere else, should remain and disrupt classes. But there are many alternatives to expulsion and suspension, alternatives that change negative behavior rather than pushing it out of view. For instance, research shows that teaching young people alternatives to violence works to prevent violence and has many other constructive side effects (Harris, 1999, 2000; Noguera, 1995). In addition, teaching young people peaceful ways to respond to conflict has longer-term benefits; it can carry over into adulthood (Bernat, 1993; Carlsson-Paige & Levin, 1985). Teaching about nonviolence and peace serves to increase prosocial behavior, reduces physical aggression, and has even been connected with improved academic achievement (Grossman et al., 1997; Harris, 1999; Stevahn, Johnson, D., Johnson, R., & Real, 1996). The only disadvantages of the use of educational measures to prevent violence involve time and image: Education is never a quick fix, and educative measures never appear to be as tough looking as expulsion, suspension, and incarceration. As a result, even *educational measures we know to be successful* are not likely to be advocated by politicians seeking to portray an I'm-tough-on-crime image.

Myth #8: Schools Are More Dangerous for Girls

Reality. Boys are more often the initiators of serious antisocial behavior, and boys are more likely to be the victims of violence in school (Olweus, 1995). In 1989 and 1995, about twice as many boys as girls between 12 and 18 years of age reported violent victimization at school, with female students about one fourth as likely to be murdered at school as male students. (Violent victimization included physical attacks or taking property directly from the student with force, weapons, or threats.)

According to the Centers for Disease Control and Prevention, male students are also more likely to have carried a weapon on school property, and males are more likely to have been threatened or injured by a weapon on school property. Males constituted 83% of all victims of school-related homicides or suicides (Centers for Disease Control and Prevention, 1999). Criminal justice professor Daniel Lockwood (1997) looked at violence in middle schools and high schools, finding that violence involved more boys than girls, yet "the average number of incidents per student was about the same" for boys as for girls. He found that "boys tended to fight mainly with other boys," but "girls were involved in almost as many fights with boys as with other girls." Curiously, "girls were the offenders in all incidents in which knives were used" (p. 3).

Girls may feel less safe in school than boys (Astor, Meyer, & Behre, 1999), although a 1998 survey of 20,000 students revealed the levels of *feeling unsafe* to be similar between high school males and females (Josephson Institute on Ethics, 1999). More dramatic than gender differences, however, are racial-plus-gender differences, with black males far more likely than any other group to be victims of murder as well as victims of other forms of violent behavior inside and outside of school (U.S. Department of Justice, 1996).

Myth #9: Security Measures Such as Guards, Metal Detectors, and Video Cameras Make Schools Safer

Reality. Researchers are saying the opposite may be true. Although it is too soon to draw definite conclusions, visible signs of security along with zero-tolerance policies appear to make students feel less safe (Skiba & Peterson, 1999a). Even as the number of weapons brought to school and confiscated at school continues to drop, today's students feel less safe than ever before. Almost all American schools now restrict access to their buildings; 11% have either a security guard or metal detectors in addition to restricted access; and 3% of all schools have restricted access, a full-time security guard, and metal detector checkpoints (Snowman, Biehler, & Bonk, 2000). Nonetheless, a recent series of surveys conducted by the Horatio Alger Association of Distinguished Americans found that the number of public school students who said they always feel safe at school dropped from 44% in 1998 to 37% in 1999 (Glassner, 1999). The enforced wearing by students and staff of identification cards or badges has raised opposition from student groups and civil-liberties organizations. In several states, students have reacted in strong opposition to the badges that display their name and usually their photograph and sometimes their Social Security numbers.

Education professor Anne Westcott Dodd (2000) asks

> How much will video cameras and police patrols help when a student feels like an outsider . . . when a student who typically responds to school authorities with hostility feels like a prison inmate as he enters the school each day? (p. 26)

Moreover, the nonhostile student will also feel threatened or unsettled by visible signs of security. Professor Dodd concludes that "locked doors and uniformed officers may make the school more secure but will probably do little to make individual students feel safe" (p. 26).

Myth #10: Aggressive Children Usually Turn Out Just Fine as Adults

Reality. They usually do not, and this is one of the clearest findings we have as well as one of the outcomes we can do much more to prevent. Aggressive behavior by a young child is one of the surest predictors of criminality at age 18. In a study of aggressive behavior over time, children were observed on multiple occasions interacting with a familiar peer at age 2. They were then observed again 3 years later. The researchers found that high levels of aggression and dependency at age 2 were significant predictors of antisocial behavior at age 6. They found that problematic behaviors were both more frequent and more stable over time for boys than for girls (Zahn-Waxler, 1987).

Patricia Chamberlain, director of parenting and foster care programs for the Oregon Social Learning Center, said that intervention must begin at an early age: "We know that if a child is being aggressive in the first grade, they're not likely to grow out of it" (Storring & Zaritsky, 2000, n.p.). The Center began a study in 1983 to assess the role of parenting on children's behavior and to see, later on in life, what effect early behavior has on later development. The children-subjects are now in their twenties, and the results are dramatic: Of those children with behavior problems in the fourth grade (including fighting, stealing, or lying), almost half had been arrested by age 14. Within that group of children with early arrest records, 75% were repeatedly arrested at least three times by the time they reached 18 years of age. Dan Olweus's extensive international research into bullying clearly shows that bullying behavior starts early, and unless there are systematic efforts to change that behavior, bullying behavior persists rather strongly. Olweus (1995) found that "35% to 40% of boys who were characterized as bullies in Grades 6 through 9 had been convicted of at least three officially registered crimes by the age of 24," but this was the case with only 10% of boys who were not identified as bullies in Grades 6 through 9 (p. 196). If there is one area that begs early intervention, it is this.

Summary

Myths about schools and violence persist despite, in many cases, an abundance of countervailing evidence. Having entered the new century, we appear to have come to the time when we should move away from myths and move away from measures that do little or nothing to reduce antisocial and violent behavior. Threatening children and adolescents with imprisonment and with suspension from school is ineffective, particularly for those at whom such strong measures are directed. Although most world cultures hold that it is a parent's responsibility to teach children prosocial behavior, blaming parents when they fail is a futile pursuit. Similarly, we should hold schools accountable; yet viewing schools as sources of violence or blaming schools for the escalation of violent behavior is counterproductive, because schools hold the greatest potential of any public or private institutions for providing a solution. It is time to refocus on what we know about children and children's behavior and about how children are socialized. For several thousand years, children have learned prosocial behavior from those around them, not from abstract, written laws and litigation, and not from sedative medication. This refocus on socialization is within our capability, for we have today reached a point at which we have an absolute abundance of both anecdotal and research information in the fields of behavioral medicine, sociology, psychology, education, and human development.

We must put together what we know about human development and human socialization, and develop a community-based social narrative with schools and educators as its change agent. Author and educator Neil Postman (1993) emphasizes this important aspect of a narrative, saying it "provides meaning . . . it is a story whose principles help a culture to organize its institutions, to develop ideals, and to find authority for its actions" (p. 172). Whereas religious groups and organizations provided in the past (and continue to provide) narratives for their members and their young persons, there must now be an initiative toward a national, nonsectarian and nonpolitical, inclusive and school-centered social narrative—a shared belief system—that prizes not only academic skills but also, and more important, prosocial behavior. This narrative will not only be the most effective solution to antisocial behavior and violence, but it will also be the only durable solution. We take the first step toward developing this narrative by moving away from myths, as I have attempted to do in this chapter. We then must define what we hope to foster through our schools, asking, "What does it mean to be educated?" "What does it mean to be socialized?" and finally, *"What can and must our schools do about antisocial and violent behavior?"* I plan to address these important questions in the next three chapters.

Social Behavior

*Psychological, Philosophical,
and Practical Bases*

Although the important roles played by home and community in the socialization of children have generally been recognized in Western culture, only relatively recently has the role played by school been acknowledged as an important force in socialization. Much of the credit for this state of affairs rests with pioneer educators such as Maria Montessori, who spoke of the importance of education as a socialization process. As the first Italian woman to have earned a doctor of medicine degree (in 1894), Montessori designed an ongoing, natural, prosocial school system that was effective, yet so subtle that it deceived many observers. She achieved success in educating Roman children who had been dismissed as being hopelessly unteachable. Her goal was clear: Montessori knew that education was essentially a social enterprise, and she geared her method toward that end. So instead of emphasizing rote memorization of facts meaningless to the students, Montessori cleverly drew on the socializing qualities of home, school, peers, and community and synthesized them into a highly controlled, structured environment, yet one that permitted students to choose many of their activities. She defined the teacher as an observer instead of authoritarian figure. Observers asked Montessori how her pupils could possibly learn, given the nondominant role of the Montessori directress (teacher) and the deemphasis on traditional memorization. Furthermore, how could children have a social life when they did so much on their own? The observers failed to see the indirect yet powerful socializing capability of the classroom environment she had set up. Montessori saw the power of the peer group in socialization, knowing that academic success and socialization are intertwined: "But what is social life," she asked, "if not the solving of social problems, behaving properly and pursuing aims acceptable to all?" (Montessori, 1988, pp. 204-205). Throughout the last century, Montessori's understanding of a child's social life, and her other innovations, gradually spread to schools throughout the world. Public, private, and religious schools adopted many of her methods and materials and her philosophy of socialization as education.

However, as we have entered the new century, it appears that industrialized nations are moving toward educative models that emphasize not socialization but correctives: attempts to fix or remedy something after the fact. Medication, for instance, has gradually been perceived to be an increasingly useful treatment to control students' antisocial behavior; in some cases, it has been seen as a panacea. Even more widespread than medication, the corrective value of litigation—specifically, criminal-justice measures—has come to be seen as an antidote for social problems. Although medical and legal measures may be fitting responses to antisocial behavior and violence, once those behaviors have occurred, such reactive measures stand apart from the preventive (and thus educative or teaching) measures necessary for human socialization.

Of course, prevention is quite different from reaction. In a discussion of primary prevention, the authors of a U.S. Institute of Mental Health report defined prevention as action "directed toward reducing the incidence of a highly predictable undesirable consequence" (Klein & Goldston, 1977, p. vii). Although some violent behaviors are unpredictable and thus not preventable, much is to be gained by taking action before the fact, particularly when it comes to human behavior. Prevention is deeply embedded in the process of socialization. A major study in the United States in the 1970s showed the dramatic value of teachers' preventive efforts on students' long-term behavior. In the Kansas City School Behavior Project, 60 teachers received intensive training in ways to foster socialization in their students. When the researchers looked at the changes in student behavior over time and across variables of race, sex, and ethnic classification, they found positive differences over time and concluded "that you could do something about what happens to a child in high school, in terms of social behavior, by teaching certain skills to a sixth-grade teacher" (Hartley, 1977, p. 72). Certainly, the successful element here may not have been what these 60 teachers did; it seems more likely that they were focused on socialization and emphasized it broadly through their interactions with students.

Socialization

Socialization has been defined as "the process whereby children become members of a social group (or the community), in the sense that they learn to behave according to the values and norms of the group or community" (Prinsloo & Du Plessis, 1998, p. 11). This membership includes both intimate and impersonal experiences in working and participating in groups. Socialization is an essential component in learning to become human. It is "the general process by which the individual becomes a member of a social group," which includes "learning all the attitudes, beliefs, customs, values, roles, and expectations of the social group" (Craig, 1983, p. 12). It is truly a universal process.

Although there are cultural differences between and within different nations, there are basic and universal similarities in the way all children are socialized. This cross-cultural similarity is especially true in the acquisition of prosocial behavior. Eisenberg and Mussen (1989) write that although many behaviors and values are specific to one's culture, "Membership in a cultural group can account only for general tendencies; it cannot be used to explain individual variations within a culture in the propensity to act prosocially" (p. 32). The authors emphasize that prosocial behavior emerges from the child's socialization experiences, which encompass all the child's interactions with parents (whom they call the most significant agents of socialization), peers, teachers, and the mass media. "These socialization experiences are critical in molding the child's prosocial disposition" (Eisenberg & Mussen, 1989, p. 33). In addition, "The child or young person is educated in particular social relationships and social situations for adequate social life, from interpersonal interaction to international coexistence" (Prinsloo & Du Plessis, 1998, p. 4). As parents, educators, and members of society, we intend for these educational efforts to be prosocial, that is, oriented toward the good of society, and this holds true across cultures. A society that does not foster prosocial behavior toward its own members cannot thrive, and may not survive.

Émile Durkheim (1961) emphasized that in order for children to learn prosocial behavior, they must first become oriented toward the well-being of others. He wrote that "moral behavior demands an inclination toward collectivity" (p. 233). In other words, before we can teach children good behavior, we must first instill in them an orientation (inclination) toward the well-being of others. Furthermore, socialization implies that some focus must be outer: on other persons, on what Durkheim called *collectivity*. This inclination toward collectivity is the necessary precondition for socialization to begin and to develop. It is important to point out that medicinal and legalistic responses do little or nothing to advance one's inclination toward collectivity. Neither through the administration of medicine nor through the imposition of criminal sanctions will a child or adolescent become oriented toward the well-being of others or toward herself or himself.

Asocialization: The Downside of Legalism

Legalism, which holds law as the supreme authority (as in *the rule of law*), is the dominant social philosophy today in the United States and other Western nations. Founded by Han Feizi over 2,000 years ago, legalism served to unify China, and it served to advance the economic interests of the United States and western Europe in the 19th and 20th centuries. Legalism has three components: *fa* (law), *shi* (legitimacy), and *shu* (arts of the ruler) (deBary, Chan, & Tan, 1960; Fung, 1966, chap. 3). Under *fa,* the law becomes written law and publicized. *Fa* also means that the state could endure irrespective of the talents or whims of the ruler (the rule of law, not of individual men and women). *Fa* relies on prescribed punishments to enforce the written word. *Shi,* or legitimacy, places great emphasis on the power within the position and not the person, who only derives power from the position he or she holds. Unlike traditional Eastern Confucianism and Western idealism—philosophies that empowered the wise individual—legalism empowered the position held by the ruler and did not honor any special personal, intellectual, or physical qualities a given ruler may have possessed. Powers inherent in the roles (positions) of parents, teachers, judges, U.S. presidents, and so forth, are examples of *shi.*

The third component of legalism, *shu,* moves questions of right and wrong and questions of human nature outside the scope of relevance: What is moral, is legally irrelevant. *Shu* permits legalism to reach a conclusion (verdict) that is apart from any moral connection or any pronouncement of rightness or wrongness of the behavior in question. For example, O. J. Simpson and Lizzie Borden (among many others) were tried and found not guilty of murder; whether they actually killed anyone was unconnected to the criminal charge of murder, thus not relevant to the jury's verdict. The rightness or wrongness of Lizzie's and O. J.'s behavior was never an issue, either. In such cases, "Law and procedures become ends in themselves and substantive goals are lost in mechanical adherence to form" (Neal & Kirp, 1986, p. 344).

Whereas Confucianism looks to tradition and constructs and maintains a narrative incorporating virtue, love of humanity, and the wisdom of ancestors, legalism uses the past only to the extent that it has produced precedents, useful underpinnings for the present day's written legal code. After Han Feizi's legalism forcibly unified China, legalism gradually faded, with China becoming a Confucian state for almost 2,000 years, until its 20th-century return to legalism. (Both capitalism and communism incorporate *fa, shi,* and *shu.*) In Western cultures, since the Enlightenment in the 18th century, legalism has been the dominant philosophy, serving the ends of government, business, and organized religion, giving credence and legitimacy to the tenets of federalism and incorporation, and ultimately, to itself.

In practice, legalism is asocial. It does not advocate or promote any human bond or social interaction within a family or community. Legalism does not recognize ethical or moral responsibilities of persons to one another, and it cannot honor human attributes such as wisdom, character, kindness, and empathy. Legalism can only define justice, for example, in terms of what can be measured, such as amounts of money, years in prison, or days or weeks suspended from school. Legalism cannot acknowledge unwritten connections inherent in the parent-child or student-teacher bonds. As a parent, the law and legal system can compel me to provide financial support for my children, but the law is silent on whether I, as a parent, should be kind or loving toward them. I have power because I am in the position of a parent, not because I am a wise person or one who cares deeply for a child's health or happiness. *Shi* with *shu.*

In their book *Vain Hopes and False Promises: The Limits of Law-Based School Reform,* Todd DeMitchell and Richard Fossey (1997) observe that "legal mandates may be effective at prohibiting actions, but they typically are poor at facilitating the adoption of new behavior, attitudes, and beliefs—the core of true educational reform" (p. xi). This is because legalism is incongruous with and antagonistic to the process of educating, of human learning. Children do not acquire new behavior from laws (*fa*). Children learn social behavior not from the position of a teacher, any teacher (*shi*), but from Ms. Jackson, who is a wise, intelligent woman, worthy of emulation, because she is a good person who holds high expectations for her students' social behavior and academic achievement. Her goodness is not irrelevant (*shu*) but essential to the very reason children want to be near her, in her class, and in some or many ways, to be like Ms. Jackson.

Cognitive learning theorists Jean Piaget and Lawrence Kohlberg established that children construct their sense of right and wrong from their social experiences: through interacting with others and by imitating the behavior of others. Children—especially young children—do not learn moral values from rules and laws, which they see as being external to themselves. Young people learn social behavior (prosocial and antisocial) from models and from expectations provided by others close to and important to children, such as members of the family and friends. As the child grows, this influential group enlarges to include unrelated people (like teachers and peers) and imaginary relationships with attractive characters (such as sports and entertainment figures). Thus in order for our schools to become more effective in the socialization and education of young people, the new social narrative must emphasize the qualities of the people within those schools, recognizing the important impact those qualities have on student behavior and achievement. In her potential contribution to student socialization, Ms. Jackson's personal traits and character are far more important than her teaching license, her advanced degrees, or her number of years of teaching experience.

Primary Socialization: The Role of the Home

Human socialization takes place through two agents that transmit and reinforce human behavior and values (Allais & McKay, 1995, p. 126): primary socialization, which includes the family and home, and secondary socialization, which is provided by schools, peer groups, and the media. The first social relationship of each child lies within the family; it is the parent-child bond. From the very first hours of life, an infant engages in behaviors that complement and become synchronized with actions of the parent (Gormly, 1997; Reissland, 1988). This I-you relationship (also called attachment) is a tie of affection that the infant forms with one specific adult caregiver (usually, the birth mother) that binds them together in space, endures over time, and fosters survival (Bowlby, 1980, pp. 39-41). This bond forms the foundation for future social development by creating a secure base from which the infant can explore the physical and social environment and gradually develop a sense of autonomy. Ultimately, "the relationship between parent and child is characterized by a common orientation toward a common goal, namely the child's becoming an adult" (Prinsloo & Du Plessis, 1998, p. 7). This relationship is bidirectional; the child and parent are each oriented toward and attracted to the other, and the way the child responds to the parent will in turn influence the way the parent reacts to the child.

The trusting I-you relationship not only provides the child with physical security but also marks the beginning of the child's social education. This denotes "awakening a positive attitude to fellow human beings and awakening a sense of . . . social conscience" (Prinsloo & Du Plessis, 1998, p. 11). This awakening of an inclination toward prosocial behavior is facilitated by a secure maternal attachment. As children grow, they move on to display this inclination toward other, nonparental adults. In sum, if the primary relationship is affectionate and nurturing, the child is more likely to imitate the parent's or teacher's prosocial behavior when interacting with others (Eisenberg & Mussen, 1989, p. 78). Studies of the outcomes of parenting on African adolescents reveal that this prosocial effect probably decreases as children age. Mboya (1995) found that children's distance and the independence they want from parents increases as children grow, yet girls' relations with parents remain generally closer than the relationship of adolescent boys and their parents.

The family is also a formidable shaper of children's self-concept, and for girls, the family may be an especially strong factor in the development of self-concept. Two researchers looked at factors affecting the self-concepts of South African students at three South African high schools in the province of the Eastern Cape (Marjoribanks & Mboya, 1998). They found that prominent variables for self-concept were based in family social status, most essentially, the number of parents in the family and the quality of family housing. For girls in the study, self-concept was defined not only by their interest and involvement in school but also by their interactions with their families. The authors concluded that family macrosocial structure, proximate family settings, and each student's personal responsibilities had moderate-to-strong associations with the adolescents' self-concepts.

The role of the family in socialization is augmented by positive and supportive early efforts from outside the family. These can be extended to help the family toward developing the young child's potential to be a positive force in society. Eric Atmore (1993, 1994) has described South Africa's Early Childhood Education and Care (EDUCARE) programs. Atmore tells how the community works with parents and how the communities, by acting as a united force, assume both the right to participate and the responsibility for participating in the political, educational, cultural, and collective matters that concern them. In the United States, Project Head Start serves a function similar to that of South Africa's EDUCARE. Research into the effects of early childhood education through Project Head Start has shown that social skills learned early in childhood are quite durable. Even for those Head Start children whose academic gains eventually faded, social and prosocial skills they acquired through Head Start stayed with them through childhood, adolescence, and into adulthood (Whitmire, 1994). In addition to availing themselves and their children of formal programs, such as EDUCARE and Head Start, parents, teachers, and caregivers can do a great deal personally to prevent violent behavior: "(1) give children consistent love and attention; (2) ensure that children are supervised and guided; (3) model appropriate behaviors; (4) do not hit children; and (5) be consistent with rules and discipline" (Massey, 1998, p. 3).

Moving from primary to secondary socialization, it is tempting to consider how closely the findings about the effects of uninvolved parents on children might apply to the effects of uninvolved teachers on their pupils, or the effects of the unavailability of schools to children. This is particularly relevant given the situation in many parts of the world where unprepared and uneducated adults are hired as teachers on a temporary or permanent basis, usually to fill a vacancy that is difficult to fill and poorly paid. The U.S. Department of Education released a report that revealed that this teacher shortage is worsening within the United States. "One of the report's more disturbing findings showed that teachers' aides rather than qualified teachers were teaching many students in Title I schools" (Wong, 2000, p. 14): schools that qualify for Title I money because their students are achieving at lower levels. The most disadvantaged American children were increasingly less likely to get qualified teachers, despite $8 billion allocated annually to this Title I program. In the economically poorest of

American schools, only 10% of aides had a bachelor's degree. This state of affairs is even more widespread in some developing and third-world nations, compounded by the fact that an impoverished child's chances of simply attending any school are practically nil (Bollag, 1999/2000; Grey, 2000).

Secondary Socialization: The Role of the School

Historically, schools have emphasized academic instruction, yet they have also been key agents of socialization, complementing the role of parents and community. The importance of the role of school in socialization has been confirmed by governmental action in establishing public schools and, in many cases, by mandating attendance by children. In Great Britain and the United States, compulsory education took root in the 19th century, and since that era, other nations, including third-world nations, have sought to improve their societies through compulsory education. (In effect, compulsory education has always existed through the educative actions of parents and community members teaching children language, life skills, and prosocial behavior.) Compulsory education has more recently come to Asian and African countries. Recently, Nigerian president Olusegun Obasanjo instituted Universal Basic Education (UBE), a compulsory and free education program for all Nigerian children from age 6 through 15, because the nation's previous system of education slipped rapidly during the 1990s (Reuters, 1999).

Even in nations with a relatively long tradition of compulsory education, a strong connection has existed between a child's readiness for school and the preliminary education (socialization) done by the parents and community prior to the child's attendance. In describing the many major forces that have shaped schools, Badenhorst (1998) points out that, until recently, schools could assume (and did assume) that all children who entered school were well prepared and ready for the socialization to be undertaken by the school. In most nations of the world, upper-class and middle-class children had (and still have) an advantage of support from the home and community that working-class children lacked. As a result, these latter children either dropped out of school or simply did not acquire maximum benefits from their schooling. This is still the case today, where, for example, economically poorer states in the United States such as South Carolina,

Louisiana, and Georgia have a much lower high school completion (graduation) rate than wealthier states. In several poorer states, a little more than half of all students graduate from high school, whereas in other, wealthier states, almost 9 out of 10 students graduate from high school. Schools and school districts respond to this disparity by encouraging all U.S. students to stay in school until graduation. Although there are drawbacks to such a sweeping advocacy of high school completion for all, from the viewpoint of socialization, the socializing value of schools can only be realized if students are in attendance at school.

In South Africa, the schools' socialization role has recently been advanced through a commitment to staff schools with personnel whose roles foster socialization, namely, guidance personnel. The National Education Policy Act of 1967 marked the commencement of guidance services for South African students. In its early years, this service was delivered in an inequitable manner across different educational departments created during apartheid, namely, the House of Representatives for colored affairs, the House of Assembly for white affairs, the House of Delegates for Asian affairs, and the Department of Education and Training for black affairs (Berard, Pringle, & Ahmed, 1997). Furthermore, guidance services were not included in the black education system until 1981. While this situation is more equitable today, the socialization gaps between South Africa's white and black schools "continue to be hindered by fiscal inequalities and political violence" (Constas, 1997, p. 682).

Two reports have detailed a lack of effective facilities and training for South African guidance personnel. These reports were issued by the Human Sciences Research Council (HSRC) in 1981 and the National Education Policy Investigation (NEPI) in 1992. Both reports pointed out that in addition to poor training for school guidance personnel, there were limitations on the time guidance teachers have to spend with individuals and groups as well as shortages of specialized personnel and materials (HSRC, 1981; NEPI, 1992). In an examination of high school counseling resources available on the Cape Peninsula, investigators in 1997 concluded that little change was noted despite the two reports (Berard et al., 1997). The guidance teacher-to-pupil ratio was 1 to 897, and even given this poor ratio, full-time guidance teachers spent about half their time in administrative tasks and formal teaching.

Some have referred to this state of affairs as a national disaster (Novicki, 1991), pointing out a severe shortage of classroom space for South African black students, as the black population of school-age children has been increasing at rates higher than the white population. By 1991, spending on schools serving black children had increased, but by 1996, money allocated for black students was 147% below the amount spent on white students. Further inhibiting the socialization value of schools has been the fact that the student dropout rate is so high for black students. Landman (1992) claims that 1 out of every 6 black children leaves school during the first year of schooling and does not ever return, and 40% of all black students leave after completing only 3 years of school. With this situation, schools cannot effectively carry out socialization, particularly for black children and adolescents. (For more information on the nature and effects of apartheid on South African education, see the annual South African Institute of Race Relations *Race Relations Surveys,* more recently titled *South African Survey,* published since 1935 by the Institute in Johannesburg.) A parallel situation exists in the United States. Although the degree of difference between black and white schools is not as dramatic as in South Africa, the well-publicized efforts of the U.S. government to integrate its public schools beginning with the 1954 *Brown versus Topeka Board of Education* Supreme Court ruling and continuing through the 1970s have not been, on the whole, very successful (Zigler & Seitz, 1982). Today, the racial disparity continues to exist in the United States and in every multiracial nation in the world.

Four Views on Schooling

What makes this pervasive inequity in world schools most tragic is the fact that schools are potentially and actually very valuable assets for the children, for their families, and for society at large. Schools are valuable not only because children tend to be physically safe in schools but also because they are places in which children can be socially safe as well. There are several different theoretical perspectives on the role of the school in the socialization of children and adolescents. Badenhorst (1998) describes four views: functionalist, conflict, interpretivist, and complexity. Functionalist theory holds that each person and group plays a part in the system viewed as a whole, and each part is viewed in terms of its function or purpose within the entire system. Socialization in that view seeks to have students "adapt to the economic, political and social institutions of their society" (Badenhorst, 1998, p. 59). American and other Western nations' school systems have emphasized functionalist theory, ranging from the most recent testing-and-standards movement back to the pragmatic, essentialist origins of educational systems that placed emphasis on pragmatic rather than social or idealistic concerns. South African governments (indeed, most nations' governments) followed functionalist ideas about policy. The education system reflected clear objectives of the government, which mandated that the various South African ethnic groups develop separately, as exemplified by limits placed on secondary education in nonwhite areas and by legislation such as the 1953 Bantu Education Act. With respect to violent and antisocial behavior, the functionalist approach emphasizes the schools' main objective: to transmit clear expectations to children for behavior (as well as academic achievement) and to back up those expectations with consequences. The recent emphases on medication and criminal-justice measures reflect a functionalist approach to schooling.

Conflict theory assumes that a tension exists within society, brought about by competing interests of individuals and groups. The theory describes, on one hand, the *haves*: those who hold power in a society through wealth, material goods, and the possession of privilege and influence. On the other side are the *have-nots,* who are constantly seeking a larger share of society's wealth and are opposed by the group in power. Research in conflict theory indicates that this tension results from conflict that is inherent in, for example, capitalist societies. For instance, access to wealth is highly controlled and limited. Because schools are controlled by the wealthy, they play a key role in this sorting and selecting process. Marxist interpretations of conflict theory might point out that U.S. public schools are even more racially segregated today, in the year 2000, than they were during the 1960s; following years of school integration legislation and civil rights initiatives, the gap (conflict) between the wealthy class and the underclass is large. Conflict theory also holds that today's greater degree of segregation in American schools is maintained by patterns of migration and mobility within the United States, typically by those with the financial resources to move to desirable, relatively crime-free and racially homogeneous areas (de facto segregation), which are usually mostly white suburban communities. Because they have little money or power, the poor remain in the inner cities and in the older, less desirable suburbs, with a resulting increase in school crimes and neighborhood and school violence in their communities.

A third view on how schools socialize children is the interpretivist point of view. This emphasizes a scientific approach involving observation of social behavior that imitates the observation of natural, physical events by scientists. The ability to interpret one's surroundings is a central task of this approach. It is understood that what is taken as normal in one cultural context may be taken differently in another cultural context. Thus the main task of this perspective is not to come up with universal principles that govern interpretation but "to uncover the specific framework that defines the rules and meanings of cultural life for a specific social group" (Badenhorst, 1998, p. 74). This approach would look into the causes (and solutions) to violence and antisocial behavior as to what each meant within the context of the culture within which it is occurring.

Last is the complexity view, which sees a world in which relationship is the essential factor in determining what is observed and how events manifest themselves. Schools are conceptualized as being fluid, organic institutions, instead of discrete, mechanistic structures as in the functionalist view. In the complexity view, the more we attempt to define what we mean by schools, the more difficult and particularistic our definitions appear to be. In applying this theory to schools, we see how the status quo is not accepted but questioned. For although the socialization objectives of the complexity view are similar to those of the functionalist view, the means to achieve those objectives differ. In the complexity view, there is no prescribed, mechanical way to improve the whole by attending to separate, unrelated parts. The complexity view recognizes that chaos exists in all schools. The traditional, functionalist response to chaos is legalistic: We restore order through control, for through the initiating of rules and prescribed punishments, we will fix the whole. Accordingly, when students exhibit antisocial behavior, it is by functionalist definition, unlawful and illegal, criminal behavior. Thus the solution arrives along with the definition of the problem. After the problem has been defined as unlawful, the solution to criminal behavior can only be composed of the linear steps of detection, arrest, trial, and punishment, or other consequences. Thus to reduce crime in School A, we need to take the first steps (detection and arrest), and we do so by instituting or increasing the presence of police and security guards, metal detectors, and strip searches of students, all of which are also viewed as deterrents to crime.

However, if the issues of antisocial behavior and violence were to be reframed and seen in the broader, complexity perspective involving numerous systems occurring at once, we may be open to a richer, more holistic, and more accurate perception of the role of schools in socialization. Of course, it is difficult to transcend functionalist perception, because educational institutions in Western nations have a tradition, derived from scientific realism and logical positivism, that holds that truth is verifiable, and the whole is the sum of its parts. By extension, if there is something wrong or amiss, in the functionalist view, we should focus on the particular part—in this case, antisocial behavior. The danger with this functionalist interpretation is that we are missing the forest for the trees or not seeing the social context within which students grow. Hence to begin to understand the socialization provided by the school (including the teaching of prosocial behavior), we must first see the school as a richly complex environment and consider what teacher and students do within that environment. A recent letter writer to the editor of the *New York Times* expressed her priorities for a social context needed for children who are faced with poor home and parenting conditions in the United States:

> This country places so little value on teachers and social workers that they are the poorest paid professionals of all. Let's put families at the Center of our social order and place high value on those who work with families and children. Instead of putting children in the most run-down, dilapidated buildings in our communities, let's build schools that we can be proud of in every neighborhood. Let's not leave it up to the poor people who live in poor neighborhoods—and then blame them for not taking better care of their children! It takes caring and money. (King, 2000, p. 19)

Collective Efficacy:
The Force Within Each Community

Just as the school is this potentially alive, complex environment, so, too, is the neighborhood or community, which is "a group of people who live within specific geographic boundaries at a certain point in time and who have cultural commonalties, collective activities and interests, and an identity of their own" (Prinsloo & Du Plessis, 1998, p. 38). Communities form an integral part of the social narrative of the role of schools in human socialization. Unfortunately, this narrative has weakened and has been transformed from the past when it implied strong ties of kinship and family. Communities have generally become depersonalized through forces such as increasing bureaucratization of levels of government and increasing centralization of power and authority.

In the United States, many are surprised to learn that their local public school's locally elected school board is really under the full authority and control of a higher, centralized state board of education. In this sense, local or community control of neighborhood schools is, in reality, a myth. Perhaps the ultimate example of a lack of community control of education is the state of Hawaii, which consists of one school district, and that is the entire state of Hawaii!

Although the role of the community has changed and has become more complex, the community can still have a powerful socializing effect. An ongoing study by the Harvard School of Public Health is examining the causes of violence, crime, and antisocial behavior in Chicago, third largest city in the United States. So far, the study (which is scheduled to continue until 2003) has surveyed 343 Chicago neighborhoods, and almost 9,000 residents have been interviewed. The researchers looked closely at neighborhoods in inner-city Chicago that at first glance, seemed similar in that they were predominantly black and impoverished. Yet the researchers soon discovered that some of these neighborhoods had significantly lower levels of crime and violent behavior than other neighborhoods with exactly the same racial balance and exactly the same poverty levels.

Their explanations for this finding are quite interesting: They found "lower rates of violence and antisocial behavior in urban neighborhoods with a strong sense of community and values" (Butterfield, 1997, p. 27). Dr. Fenton Earls, the director of the study, identified the presence of informal social control through which residents themselves act to achieve public order rather than relying on external control (police crackdowns, for example). Informal social control was also an example of what the authors called "collective efficacy," which is the "willingness (of residents) to intervene and control group level processes and visible signs of social disorder, providing a key mechanism influencing opportunities for interpersonal crime in a neighborhood" (Sampson, Raudenbush, & Earls, 1997, p. 918). This collective efficacy on the behalf of residents enabled them to reduce truancy, discourage the painting of graffiti, and many other antisocial acts. This finding is significant because it identifies factors other than those traditionally connected with resultant violence and antisocial behavior (e.g., poverty, racial discrimination, unemployment) and points to the importance of informal, internal, neighborhood controls instead of externally imposed rules, laws, and sanctions.

Sociology professor Robert Sampson explained the Chicago study's findings in more detail. He said the prosocial phenomenon of collective efficacy does not necessarily arise from personal or familial ties but comes about in the presence of a narrative, "a shared vision . . . a fusion of a shared willingness of residents to intervene and social trust, a sense of engagement and ownership of public space" (Butterfield, 1997, p. 27). Certainly, unemployment and poverty make it difficult to achieve and maintain community cohesion to the point at which adults will intervene in the lives of children, but the Chicago study's findings highlight promising directions toward a shared social narrative in the quest to develop solutions for violent and antisocial behavior in children. In a study involving the U.S. Department of Education, the U.S. Department of Justice, and the National School Safety Center, the Centers for Disease Control and Prevention (1999) summarized its report by stating that "the full involvement of the community is critical to developing a sense of ownership for the problem of violence and its solutions" (n.p.).

Communities, Schools, and Human Needs

Looking at the Chicago study through the lens of socioeducation, we should find little cause for surprise. When we speak of social interventions, we are referring to interpersonal communication, the central concept of socioeducation. The informal control exerted by the community was successful through effective communication. Prinsloo and Du Plessis (1998) describe communication as "the interactive process through which thoughts, opinions, feelings or information are transferred from one person to another with the intention to inform, to influence or to elicit a reaction" (p. 9). Interventions that bring about socialization in the community are forms of communication, but they are also, in effect, means of teaching. The community in this sense is a school in macrocosm—as schools and classrooms within schools are communities in microcosm.

Like the urban Chicago neighborhoods that showed cohesion, classrooms create and spread the glue of social cohesion on a person-to-person level. Teacher interventions within those classrooms may be either verbal or nonverbal, involving words, gestures, physical contact, or other combinations of words and action. In any form, teacher interventions are most effective in building social glue when they are made before the fact of antisocial behavior. That is, teacher interventions are most effective when they serve to prevent misbehavior and when they serve to support and reinforce ongoing, prosocial behavior (DiGiulio, 2000, pp. 61-62). This is true even when we consider positive interventions by other students. By any measure, teachers and schools (and communities) do not work best as corrective, punitive enterprises. The community—whether it is defined as a neighborhood or a cultural group or both—has its greatest consequence in socialization by providing a secure context for communication. Such a context serves well its individual members and family groups. In "Positive Approaches to Violence Prevention: Peace Building in Schools and Communities," a conference held at Indiana University, one of the key themes to emerge was that "Communication is the key hurdle to preventing violence" (Plucker, 2000, p. 3). An essential part of effective violence-prevention programs was "a strong communication skills component" including teaching students how to communicate, how to listen and talk effectively in an increasingly technological world (p. 3).

In addition to fostering communication, the school contributes to the fulfillment of human needs through its social context; met needs are essential elements in the child's development. In Maslow's hierarchy of human needs, the fulfillment of higher-level growth needs (such as the quest for knowledge, beauty, and self-growth), require that lower-level, deficit needs must first be met (Maslow, 1970). In order from lowest to highest, these needs include survival and physiological needs, safety needs, belonging and love needs, and a need for self-esteem. The most basic need for survival includes the need to be fed and sheltered. Although this most basic need is generally well met in first-world nations, in which in-school lunch and breakfast programs exist for children whose family income is low, this is not the case in third-world schools and communities. It is an increasing problem in industrialized nations such as South Africa where, Prinsloo, Vorster, and Sibaya (1996) point out, "The percentage of children in South Africa whose basic needs are not met is growing by the day"(p. 316).

Throughout the world, even in communities in which a child's most basic survival needs are being met, the next-most-basic need—safety—is increasingly being identified as an unmet need in children and adolescents. It is all too obvious that safety needs are compromised in school when students experience antisocial and violent behavior by other students and by school staff members. The importance of safety and security has also been emphasized by Rapoport, Rapoport, and Strelitz (1977), citing Talbot's (1976, p. 171) premises, including "being needed and wanted" and "being attended to, cared for, and protected" (p. 11). Schools' failure to provide for these needs has detrimental effects on the fulfillment of students' other basic needs, namely, belonging and love needs and self-esteem needs. In turn, this will diminish the likelihood that students' higher-level needs (for self-actualization) can be realized. Ultimately, when schools themselves are seen as violent or uncaring or unsafe places, human socialization is jeopardized.

Summary

Certainly, the role of primary socialization that is carried out in the home sets the basis for prosocial and antisocial behavior. The value of schools and the community, historically significant sources in the process of socialization, has lately diminished. Legalism, along with centralization and bureaucratization, has weakened the socialization that schools once provided clearly and reliably. Nevertheless, schools represent society's best location and most efficient delivery system for turning around flawed educative efforts of the home. And within those schools as communities in microcosm, the role of teachers and the interventions made by teachers can serve to confront the problem of student antisocial behavior head-on and foster prosocial behavior. The ongoing results of the Chicago study are encouraging, in particular, the identification of the social narrative called collective efficacy should have dramatic policy and practical implications for schools and for those who occupy those schools.

As part of that school-based social narrative, the teacher must play the most central role. Research has shown that the best deterrent to school violence is the presence of a teacher, particularly when that teacher makes supportive interventions, interventions that students characterized as *caring* (Astor, Meyer, & Behre, 1999). Students' need for safety is well met by teachers who make caring interventions. These forms of teacher communication (caring interventions), along with an administrative policy that was similarly caring (gave support to teachers' interventions), were identified as the most significant contextual factors in preventing antisocial behavior in high school. The importance of teacher-student and student-teacher communication is well summed up by Prinsloo and Du Plessis (1998): "Without interpersonal communication education cannot take place. It is only through communication with their fellow man that children can achieve self-actualization, realize their social-communicative possibilities and form a self-concept" (pp. 9-10).

But in order for all this to work, a shared sense of purpose—a social narrative—must be in place. This involves an ethic of care and mutual respect, and a high value placed on human dignity and human relationships. If this narrative is not in place, it must be created. If it is neither in place nor in the process of being created, then the perfect climate exists for antisocial and violent behavior. Although, as I said earlier, schools are relatively safe places, if the social narrative is not supported, and we increasingly rely on the quick fixes suggested by legalism and medication, schools will gradually lose more and more of their caring teachers—their Ms. Jacksons—qualified teachers who hold high academic and social expectations for students, make interventions, and do not literally or figuratively turn their backs on students.

Problem Areas

Where Social Behavior Becomes Antisocial Behavior

In the past, the relationship between the individual and institutions of socialization was less complex than today: Children were socialized primarily by the mother and family in the home and, as they grew, were formally educated as well by persons associated with local institutions such as school and church. R. M. Kidder (2000) refers to this state of affairs as a "three-legged stool . . . the typical community had an ethics delivery system that rested on the three legs of home, church, and school" (n.p.). Historically, the home and family as well as peers, school, and work constituted the educative society of the child. Today, however, the influence of home and church have, to a degree, decreased; the school remains largely alone in carrying out (or attempting to carry out) much of the educative functions that in the past were shared with parents, home, and church. Kidder describes this quite colorfully: "Modern society, it appears, has kicked away the first two legs" (n.p.), leaving school as the figurative last leg of a one-legged stool. In modern society, schools now serve as the major institution "devised by the adult generation for maintaining and perpetuating the culture," providing the necessary tools for survival by transmitting values and knowledge (Ornstein & Levine, 2000, p. 277).

What Is Antisocial Behavior?

Antisocial behavior is behavior "opposed or contrary to normal social instincts or practices" (Abate, 1999, p. 39). Antisocial behavior encompasses two characteristics. First, it involves a violation of social relationships, such as community and interpersonal relationships, as well as those involving public authority. Second and more profound, all antisocial behaviors serve as "detrimental phenomena erosive to society" (van't Westende, 1998, p. 268). The damage affects the community itself and involves the offenders, their victims, and even next of kin to different degrees. Antisocial behavior influences the nature of community and national life, affecting a nation's or community's quality of life. In its extreme form, antisocial behavior becomes violence: strong "behavior that violates other individuals" (Thayer-Bacon, 1999, p. 140). In Western nations, the public fear of violent and antisocial behavior goads policymakers and legislators to redirect attention (and funds) toward crime detection, apprehension, and incarceration instead of toward education and other social services that seek to improve the quality of life of children and their families. In many Western societies, homes and business establishments have increasingly resorted to security measures, such as the installation of security fences, burglar alarms, door bolts, and the use of armored and bulletproof materials in the construction of homes and vehicles. (DuPont's Kevlar is today's miracle fiber for an unsafe world.) Because they highlight the issue of potential danger, security measures paradoxically serve to intensify human fear, which in the case of schools, interferes with learning and hinders human relationships. Speaking of this situation with regard to African American children, Prothrow-Stith and Quaday (1995) said, "When our children's ability to learn is being dangerously undermined, the foundation of our society is being damaged in a manner that cannot easily be repaired" (p. 27). Strong and highly visible security measures in schools may reinforce the idea among students (particularly minority-group students) that schools are unfriendly and adversarial as well as unsafe places.

By definition, antisocial behavior is usually directed at others, but sometimes it is self-directed and, in some extreme cases of violence, it can both be directed at others and at one's self, as in murder-suicide. Psychologist Laurence Steinberg (1999) describes this issue in terms of the presence of "internalizing" or "externalizing" disorders. The former consist of harmful behaviors that are turned inward, directed at one's self, and show themselves as depression, anxiety, or phobias. Externalizing disorders, on the other hand, show themselves as behaviors directed primarily at others, where "the young person's problems are turned outward" and result in antisocial behavior and delinquency (p. 402). Because schools are mainly educative rather than therapeutic institutions, emphasis in school is typically placed on externalizing behaviors instead of on the more subtle internalizing behaviors. Thus it is more likely that internalized disorders will be less noticeable in schools than externalized behaviors, particularly in schools that are huge and anonymous and highly competitive athletically, socially, and academically. Students whose anger is turned inward are perhaps more likely to be laughed at, belittled, taunted, and excluded in these circumstances than to be identified and treated. Hence it may be that these kinds of responses are triggers that turn the internalizing disorders of depression, anxiety, and phobia into externalizing disorders directed at others with great force and with horrific consequences.

Although all violent behavior is antisocial in nature, most antisocial behavior is not violent behavior. This is reflected in recent statistics available from the U.S. Department of Education (1998): The research sample of 1,234 principals revealed that

> during the 1996-1997 school year, student tardiness (40%), student absenteeism or class cutting (25%), and physical conflicts among students (21%) were the three discipline issues most often cited by public school principals as serious or moderate problems in their schools. (p. 12)

Fewer than 2% of this group identified more severe problems, such as the sale of drugs on school grounds, student possession of weapons, or physical abuse of teachers as either serious or moderate problems in their schools. The report concluded that in U.S. schools, violent behavior occurred at an annual rate of 53 incidents per 100,000 students. Although they show a fairly low level of violent behavior, these statistics do not reflect the widespread existence of less severe antisocial behaviors (such as incivility) and internalized disorders (such as depression, anxieties, and phobias), which are probably more prevalent in today's schools.

Two Perspectives on Antisocial Behavior

Antisocial behavior affects both the individual and the individual's social environment. On the one hand, we can perceive antisocial behavior as "a personal problem, where the causes and solutions lie within the individual and his or her immediate environment" (van't Westende, 1998, p. 262). This perspective emphasizes a psychological, individual-oriented view. Consistent with this perspective are children and adolescents who appear to lack the ability to practice self-restraint or regulate their own behavior (Feldman & Weinberger, 1994). Adolescents who lack the ability to control their impulses are described as being "undercontrolled" (Robins, John, Caspi, Moffitt, & Stouthamer-Loeber, 1996, pp. 157-171). A common solution lies in treating the individual, typically, with medication and, secondarily, through individualized therapy such as psychotherapy and, in a growing number of instances, through adjudication and incarceration. Indeed, the public stands ready to react to antisocial and violent behavior by individual children and adults. A recent statewide referendum in California revealed that 70% of voters said yes to a proposition "that would increase the number of juvenile suspects who could be arrested and put on trial as adults" ("Key California Votes," 2000). Responding to this public sentiment are political leaders such as Florida's Governor Jeb Bush, who spoke recently on the increased prison capacity for young people in Florida. He reportedly warned young people: "There is room at the inn."

In a different perspective, antisocial behavior is a social problem, one that "has its causes and solutions outside the individual and his or her immediate environment" (van't Westende, 1998, p. 262). This perspective defines antisocial behavior as an educational problem, in that its solution or resolution involves the teaching (and reteaching) of prosocial behavior. Certainly, inborn, inherited traits play a strong role influencing human behavior. We are powerless to change the physiological makeup of the individual (except, of course, through surgery). As a society, we have potentially more control over the child's social and educational milieu than we do over his or her physiological makeup. It is within school settings that we can engineer the social environment. Regrettably (from the viewpoint of socialization), American schools have emphasized the first perspective, viewing a classroom as a collection of individuals rather than as a social group. In such cases, it becomes much more difficult to teach prosocial behavior, because what is best for all (Durkheim's "collectivity") is subordinated to the individual desires of each person.

Stress and the Mass Media

As mentioned earlier, children and adolescents have always experienced stress from their family and peer relationships and from school as well as from the events in the natural, physical world. Lately, the amount of stress in society has increased. Much of this recent increase has been attributed to the mass media. (Mass media produce written and spoken words, largely through literature, radio, television, and, most recently, home computers.) Since the invention of the printing press in the early 1500s, the mass media have increasingly figured in the socialization of the world's children. Some observers have called television and other media "the first curriculum" because of the way they influence not only what we know but also how we know. Television defines attitudes toward knowledge and learning and influences socialization (Stroman, 1991; Taylor, 1998). (I was troubled as I watched television in rural Russia, seeing that it consisted largely of American and British fare featuring violence, idiotic and aggressive police, and scheming lawyers. I was more distressed when my host family's young son asked me if it was true that all Americans carried guns and dressed up for cocktail parties each evening!) As a result of its rapid growth over the past 50 years, television and its other forms (video games, the Internet) have become a larger presence in the lives of the world's children and adolescents. The capability of the mass media to entertain is well established. Yet some aspects of the mass media have been identified as being harmful, in that they transmit stress (from the macro level) into the lives of children and adolescents. For example, prior to the advent of television, children and adults were relatively unaware of environmental degradation and threats posed by nuclear weapons. Before television, children and adolescents were not able to receive violent, antisocial information, ideas, pictures, and words on demand, instantly, in great detail, and delivered directly to home or school. (They were also unaware that schools were violence-ridden, dangerous places.)

It is estimated that thousands of studies have been done examining the effect of television on children, with particular respect to children's imitation of antisocial and violent behavior that they have viewed on television. Even as early as 1950, when television was in its infancy, American parents and teachers were concerned about the effects of television violence on young children (Witty, 1950). Over the years, violent and aggressive behavior by children has been increasingly attributed to television viewing (National Institute of Mental Health, 1982; Zuckerman & Zuckerman, 1985). In a review of the body of 30 years' worth of research on how children and adolescents are affected by viewing video and televised violence, Murray (1995) identified three main ways. First is the direct-effects process, whereby children and adolescents who watch a great deal of violence tend to become more aggressive themselves and develop attitudes that favor or permit aggressive behavior as a way to settle conflicts. The second effect is desensitization, through which children who watch much televised violence become less sensitive to violence in their daily lives; they are less empathetic toward others, and they are more likely to tolerate greater levels of violence in society. People desensitized to violence are less likely to intervene when others are victims of antisocial, destructive, and violent behavior. The third effect is what Murray called the "Mean World Syndrome": Children who view much televised violence see the world as a dangerous, evil place, which causes children to become more fearful (p. 10). Certainly, the content of television has become increasingly violent, and many programs viewed by children portray violence in ways that promote imitation by children (National Television Violence Study, 1996-1998). Nevertheless, this simple focus on television as a variable may represent only part of the problem, especially when we step back and view violent behavior in a larger, global perspective.

In South Africa, Martin Botha (1995) conducted a major longitudinal study into the effects of television violence and aggression on South African children. Subjects consisted of 348 children in Grades 2 and 3. The author's researchers collected data from each child, the child's peers and parents, and school personnel through structured interviews. They looked at the influence of television, but they also considered the effects of several other variables thought to influence violent and antisocial behavior, such as poverty, educational quality, poor housing and essential facilities, as well as political issues and the replacement of the extended family in urban black communities. Botha found that television did not play as significant a role as had been anticipated. Instead, the researcher identified violent adult behavior in the community and in the home as having been more influential in fostering violent behavior in young people than television. Parental aggression and parental child-rearing practices especially influenced violent behavior by children. Botha reported that parental aggression and violence often existed together with violence in the community. Although television is a contributing factor to violent behavior, it seems clear that children and adolescents learn violent and aggressive behavior most efficiently from models provided in their real-life experiences with parents, peers, and teachers.

Attitudes toward and tolerance of violence are also deeply influenced by personally experienced violence. Unfortunately, when violence is personally experienced, young victims of violence tend to tolerate it, feel helpless to do anything about it, or even wind up approving of its use. This was borne out in a recent study conducted at the University of Durban that involved 1,000 South African student teachers. They perceived schools to be violent places, "characterised by political, state-linked, or gender violence" (Suransky-Dekker, 1997, p. 1). To the surprise of the researcher, many of these student teachers approved of corporal punishment; a typical student comment was, "I was punished and look . . . I made it to University!" (p. 2). Given the amount of violence children experience firsthand, television may be more of a scapegoat than actual villain in the teaching and learning of violent behavior.

Socioeducational Factors That Produce Antisocial Behavior

Martin Botha's (1995) longitudinal television study serves as a fine starting point for discussion of other socioeducational problem areas in contemporary society that influence children. Broadly, these problem areas include poverty, child abuse and neglect, inadequate health and welfare, and family disintegration (Squelch, 1998). In terms of their effect on the behavior of young people, these problem areas contain specific socioeducative factors that lead to the development of inappropriate social behavior identified by society as juvenile delinquency. T. R. Botha (1977) identified four socioeducational factors that foster juvenile delinquency: disturbed involvement (family disharmony), disturbed role identification (child-parent identification), disturbed social-societal relationships (peer group associations), and disturbed entry into the social environment (school factors). A brief description of each factor will help to show its influence on the social behavior of children.

Disturbed Involvement. It is said that "the family is each child's first school," and with regard to the family's educative role, that is certainly true. "Although its organization varies, the family is the major early socializing agent in every society. As such, it is the first medium for transmitting culture to children" (Ornstein & Levine, 2000, p. 278). At the core of this is the birth mother and infant bond. In all infants, the basic sense of trust versus mistrust is established soon after birth, hinging on the question of whether or not the infant will be loved, cared for, and protected from harm. This is true in all world cultures in which "it seems increasingly clear that parental rejection has 'malignant' effects for all humans" (Rohner, 1975, p. 166). Rohner adds that "the need for positive response is rooted in man's psychosocial and morphological evolution, and when we are denied love, esteem, and other forms of positive response, 'pernicious' things happen to us" (p. 166). A child can also be harmed even before birth. The health care a mother-to-be receives (or fails to receive) can affect the developing child in utero. Or the mother-to-be can be a victim of violence during her pregnancy. The newborn infant may be at serious risk of violence as well. In the shaken-baby syndrome, acute brain damage, blindness, and death can result from an adult's shaking an infant. Witnessing violent behavior in the home, being a victim of that violence, and being reinforced for aggression are significant factors in the learning of violence. In other words, violent homes generally produce violent children.

Although human-development experts disagree on the amount of aggressive behavior that is inborn compared with what is learned (the nature-versus-nurture issue), there is little disagreement that aggressive behavior appears early in life. In highly aggressive adolescent boys, for example, patterns of violent behavior are typically seen in their early childhood. In fact, one of the strongest predictors of whether or not a boy will be imprisoned by the time he is a young adult is whether or not he has shown serious antisocial or violent behavior at an early age—around 4 or 5 years of age (Buka & Earls, 1993; Zahn-Waxler, 1987). Irrespective of a child's inborn level of aggression, abusive, harsh treatment and neglect of young children create more damage and can inhibit the development of prosocial behavior. In an American study (Main & George, 1985), toddlers between 1 and 3 years of age were observed at a day-care center. Children who were themselves not abused demonstrated prosocial behaviors, such as concern, sadness, and empathy when in the presence of another distressed child, but not one child who had been abused showed any of these responses in the presence of other distressed children. In fact, the abused children responded to another child's distress with fear, anger, or aggression, responses that were almost completely absent among the nonabused group. Over time, abused children's aggressive behavior can be perpetuated by parental behavior toward the child, for "ineffective parent discipline and child anti-social behavior mutually maintain each other" (Vuchinich, Bank, & Patter-son, 1992, p. 518). A child's strongly aggressive behavior may serve as a spur to the parent to behave in an aggressive, abusive way, thus creating a self-perpetuating cycle of abuse-reaction-abuse.

Just as harsh and abusive treatment inhibits the development of pro-social behavior, uninvolvement (neglect) by parents can be just as harmful. Uninvolved parents are those not committed to being a parent, and they appear to be quite neglectful—indifferent to the child's need for affection, structure, and limits. Children of uninvolved parents show greater impul-sivity, earlier sexual behavior, greater use of drugs, and lower self-esteem (Fuligni & Eccles, 1993; Kurdek & Fine, 1994; Lamborn, Mounts, Stein-berg, & Dornbusch, 1991). From the perspective of the origins of anti-social and violent behavior, uninvolved parents most resemble actively abusive parents in that both styles tend to produce children who "are aggressive and show disagreeable behavior" (Gormly, 1997, p. 225).

Disturbed Role Identification. Children identify closely with their par-ents; they identify with the same-sex parent and with the opposite-sex parent in different ways. Educational neglect or outright abuse will damage this identification, whereas a positive role identity and a constructive relation-ship between parent and child—and between the child's two parents as well—will promote a healthy role identity in the child.

This appears to be a particular problem for boys and antisocial behav-ior. Prinsloo, Vorster, and Sibaya (1996) describe "toughening," through which a boy is expected to act like a mature man, to absorb life's punches stoically, as he avoids the show of feelings (p. 163). Both boys and girls need positive human role models, but boys particularly need positive role models, particularly because boys are less capable, in general, of forming close personal relationships by instinct (Gurian, 2000, p. 18). They need to learn from the culture—from those closest to them—how to relate amenably to others. Looking at 30 different cultures around the world, Gurian (2000) noticed a shift: Traditional ways that boys identify positively with older males are disappearing, especially during adolescence when "such guidance is most critical," leaving young men "morally neglected," surrounded with violent and sexual messages in media and music (p. 19). It must be added, however, that although boys historically identified most naturally with the behaviors of adult men, boys today can (and should be able to) acquire prosocial behaviors from their interactions with *human* role models—from women as well as men. What matters most is the quality of the adult-child relationship and not the alignment of genders. If Ms. Jackson is an excellent, caring teacher, she is so for both boys and girls.

However true this may be and however valuable human role models are, other social factors work against a child's smooth acquisition of prosocial behavior. In a study of 452 African American and European American boys in North Carolina, researchers found that the most highly aggressive boys (tough boys) were also among the most popular and socially connected of children in their schools (Rodkin, Farmer, Pearl, & Van Acker, 2000). Boys who were seen as being nice or boys who strove for academic success or boys who were deeply sensitive to the needs of others were denigrated and referred to as queer, effeminate, or gay. We also know that bullying or peer abuse by boys is often connected with role identification. Researcher Dan Olweus (1995) investigated bullying among schoolchildren in Scandinavia as well as in schools in Great Britain, Japan, the Netherlands, Australia, Canada, and the United States. He found that male bullies were usually reared by uninvolved parents who were indifferent, lacked warmth and involvement, were permissive for aggressive behavior, and used "power-assertive disciplinary techniques," such as physical punishment (p. 199). Olweus also found that 35% to 40% of boys identified as bullies in Grades 6 through 9 had been convicted of at least three crimes by the time they reached age 24, whereas this was true of only 10% of the boys who were not classified as bullies. There is little question that bullying behavior comes about through unhealthy role identification. The reverse is seen when boys have a healthy role identification provided by a significant adult model (typically, the boy's father) from whom boys learn how to treat others in prosocial and caring ways and without feeling their masculinity is compromised. This identification is especially crucial early in the boy's life. There is wisdom in the old saying, "The best gift a father can give a son is to love and respect his son's mother." It is also a fine gift to society.

Disturbed Social-Societal Relationships. Second in importance only to parents, the peer group is highly significant in its influence on child behavior, and during adolescence, it exceeds the influence of parents on the individual. Peer culture is a major socialization experience, with most students naming their friends as the best thing about their school (Goodlad, 1984, pp. 76-77). Adolescents need to see themselves as part of a peer group to help form their adult identity. In a reciprocal fashion, the peer group becomes relatively powerful in the life of the adolescent, because there is an ongoing risk of being ostracized from the group.

In its powerful and influential role, the peer group may provide a mostly positive, prosocial orientation for the individual, or it may provide more negative, antisocial direction. Van't Westende (1998) identifies several ways in which a peer group may promote or cause juvenile delinquency. First, the peer group provides a channel to greater independence, and if the group is positive, it will cultivate sound relationships. If, however, the influence is negative, antisocial behaviors will result, sanctioned by the peer group. The peer group also supplies a field of experience for social relations in which adolescents can try on identities and determine where they fit in (p. 277). During adolescence, information about oneself (self-identity) is obtained largely through the peer group.

In sum, the peer group provides a chance for the individual to play different roles and try on different identities, and if the group upholds deviant values and attitudes, the child may develop into an adult whose values and behavior will clash with those in his or her future adult community. In addition to peer group relations, individuals engage in social-societal relationships through their occupation or employment. Indeed, unemployment and underemployment are among the most challenging of social issues that face South Africa, the United States, Australia, and other industrialized nations as well as nations emerging from Communist government, such as Russia and the former republics of the Soviet Union. Journalist David Orr (1994) interviewed leading experts on South Africa who were most concerned about the economic chasm between white and black South Africans. It has been estimated that 84% of South Africa's black population earn less money than is needed to ensure adequate basic nutrition for themselves and their families. Orr stated that what is needed "are more schools, more housing, more extensive health care, and, above all, more jobs" (p. 12), particularly for the black population, many of whom are unemployed. In addition to the obvious economic need in this segment of South Africa's population, a socialization need also exists that can be facilitated by a greater and more equitable number of black South Africans entering the workforce, particularly in the upper civil service and in private business.

Disturbed Entry Into the Social Environment. Of the four socio-educational factors that foster delinquency, the child's entry into the social environment of the school holds, perhaps, the greatest promise for helping to mend, if not reverse, miseducative efforts by parents and family. Certainly, school cannot quickly or completely reverse serious misbehavior, and it cannot cure serious emotional disturbance. However, teachers and schools receive children at a young enough age so that they can reframe the child's antisocial behavior, presenting an environment emphasizing prosocial behavior. Within each classroom, a teacher can create a small society, a society in microcosm where positive behavior is valued, discussed, modeled, encouraged, and expected.

Throughout the world, when children and adolescents who live in poverty and in violent circumstances bring those circumstances to school, teachers and other educators are challenged to address the social problems that result. But even more basic to this challenge is the question of access to school by the poor. For many of the world's children, poverty prevents them from getting to school at all: It is estimated that almost 25% of all the world's children between the ages of 6 and 11 have never attended one day of school, with girls comprising almost two thirds of that number (Kielburger, 1998, p. 309). Schools cannot teach socialization or academics to children who are not present.

As mentioned earlier, AIDS represents a dire threat to millions of children, particularly in Africa and Asia, where the number of AIDS orphans will rise dramatically over the next decade. This has many ramifications, including limited educational opportunity. In parts of Africa and Asia, only about one half of all children aged 6 through 11 years were enrolled in school in 1992, yet this represented a dramatic increase from 1960 (United Nations Educational, Scientific, and Cultural Organization, 1994). Walking hand in hand with poverty, child labor or servitude afflicts 250 million children throughout the world, providing another formidable barrier to school enrollment and regular attendance. Kielburger (1998) states, "These children don't have a chance for education, to live a normal life, even a chance to play" (p. 168). Access to school, particularly for all poor children, is imperative, because universally, schools are the safest of places for children and adolescents. Children and adolescents are safer in school than working in factories or fields, safer than wandering on the streets, and safer even than being in their own homes. Children and adolescents are immensely safer in school than as a passenger in a motor vehicle or riding on a bicycle.

Schools as Oppressive Environments

On the other hand, although they are places where children are relatively safe from serious violence, schools can present an oppressive environment. In some cases, school can worsen the miseducative harm already experienced by a child, with the harm falling most heavily, again, on the child of poverty, irrespective of citizenship, race, or gender. "Unfortunately," van't Westende (1998) relates, "the school and its teachers are often responsible for creating the very climate which may lead to delinquency" (p. 275). South Africa Minister of Education Kader Asmal recently spoke of "low teacher morale" as "one of the biggest challenges we have to face," adding that violence and crime throughout the world were contributing to stressful working conditions and low teacher morale. He called on teachers to help address the problems by showing a "new professionalism," taking into account new and creative ways teachers can develop positive relationships with students as well as improve the content of learning and the materials used (Garson, 2000, n.p.).

In a very real sense, modern American public schools have become less safe places for students, because they have become safer places for aggression and for aggressive behavior. Sometimes, the adults in charge model that behavior quite clearly. Recently, 30 girls at a Connecticut middle school were strip-searched after $50 was reported missing by a student. After being threatened with arrest if they did not comply, all 30 girls removed their clothing in the presence of an assistant principal, gym teacher, and security guard. No money turned up, and the three women who conducted the strip search were suspended (Schuster, 1997). Despite the apology of the superintendent of schools and the predictable threatening of lawsuits, the harm had been done to these adolescents.

Observers of modern American public schools say that schools have grown increasingly absent of character and purpose, and those within them are allowed to behave in ways that are legal but are clearly not ethical or moral (such as strip-searching students). "Modern secular education is failing," according to Neil Postman (1993), "because it has no moral, social, or intellectual center . . ." (p. 185). He adds that "the most important contribution schools can make to the education of our youth is to give them a sense of coherence in their studies, a sense of purpose, meaning, and interconnectedness in what they learn" (pp. 185-186).

In addition to these philosophical concerns, there are practical problems as well. For example, more than in the past, today's teachers fear being sued or fear being seen as heavy-handed or authoritarian. Most worrisome are indications that teachers who attempt to convey high expectations to students—teachers who are considered to be "strict"—may be more likely to be targets of student violence than other teachers, according to a Metropolitan Life Insurance Company survey (1993, pp. 45-46).

Fifty-seven percent of American high school students surveyed said that strict teachers are the most likely victims of student aggression and violence. Given the importance of teacher clarity in the preventing of antisocial behavior, this survey result deserves further exploration. First, we need to define *strict* and understand if it implies *harsh* as well. Are these teachers likely victims because they are mean to students or because they hold high expectations for student behavior? Or do students automatically see any teacher who holds high expectations as being mean to them? It is entirely likely that this issue has emerged from an American society that embraces legalism, emphasizing the rights of the individual over the needs of the group. Hence, Ms. Jackson's clearly conveyed behavioral expectations for her class of 30 students may actually place her in jeopardy.

The Clash of Legalism and Socialization

Legalism opposes unwritten standards and behavior expectations that arise from a community (school, classroom, extended family, etc.), for they are seen as fetters to individual self-realization, or worse, they are likely to be applied unfairly. This latter notion was embodied in a recent statement by law professor Peter Rubin of Georgetown University School of Law in Washington, D.C. In responding to questions as to why no measures were taken against three Georgetown Law School students who were accused "of running an Internet stock scheme that netted almost $350,000," Professor Rubin explained that moral standards in the past were used to unfairly punish some members of society. He claimed, "We have replaced a system of community control over people's behavior with one associated with more formal procedures for ethical or legal lapses." He went on to characterize the system of "formal procedures" as "an enormous step forward for society" (Berenson, 2000, p. 16WK). I disagree and believe it is a step in the wrong direction as we ask our schools to socialize our students. Recall the three elements of legalism (*fa, shi,* and *shu*) that figure prominently in this line of reasoning. Squashing community control within neighborhoods, classrooms, or schools in favor of control by formal legal procedures (*fa*) will serve to enhance the power of the legal and criminal-justice system (*shi*); worse, it replaces a prosocial narrative with an amoral narrative (*shu*). Recall the Chicago neighborhoods study cited in Chapter 3 that showed the value of collective efficacy in lower crime neighborhoods, which were precisely those where the people in the community exerted control over—and positively influenced—the prosocial behavior of residents by deterring antisocial behavior. However, a system of formal procedures moves that control from the community or school to an external, legal elite composed of bureaucrats, legislators, lawyers, judges, special interest groups, and corporate interests. As they apply to school, formal legal procedures are unhelpful to—beyond the reach of—educators, parents, and citizens who seek to foster socialization and use community control to teach prosocial behavior.

In fact, community control had been at the heart of strong schools and classrooms across the United States and throughout the world. A prosocial system of community control is precisely what effective teachers establish within their classrooms, working from a preventive perspective instead of a blaming, formal-procedures perspective. Alternatives to this community control are bleak: either a laissez-faire, do-your-own-thing classroom that sees antisocial behaviors as legal lapses, or an authoritarian teacher dictatorship. Both alternatives are supported by legalism: The first defers to students' unfettered constitutional rights ("I can't intrude . . . I might get sued"); the second, in its definition of the powers inherent in the position of teacher (*shi*), is derived from each state's constitution and its laws (*fa*). In some cases, this power extends to the hitting of children in response to an offense. Indeed, corporal punishment provides one of the best illustrations of schools as oppressive environments, because corporal punishment continues as a legal response to school infractions in about 20 states and in many nations.

Corporal Punishment. Throughout the world, corporal punishment of young persons is a common practice used to control children's behavior and to enforce obedience. It is also a most efficient violence delivery system, whereby violent behavior is transmitted from adult to child. As such, corporal punishment represents one of the most distinctive features of a school social environment that is oppressive. Some nations, such as Sweden, Norway, Denmark, and Finland, are exceptions, because they outlaw all physical punishment of children both in school and in the home. Corporal punishment is practically unknown in Italian schools, and it has been banned in Poland for more than 200 years.

However, in many nations, corporal punishment remains a standard response to child behavior. In the West Indies, for example, corporal punishment is considered to be a routine means of disciplining children even though West Indies children are generally well loved by their parents or caretakers (Arnold, 1982). In a survey of the prevalence of corporal punishment in preparatory and secondary schools of Alexandria, Egypt, it was found that 4 out of every 5 boys (80%) had received physical punishment by teachers, and over 61% of female students had incurred physical punishment. The reasons for administering corporal punishment included both as a response to student antisocial behavior and as a consequence for poor academic achievement (Youssef, Attia, & Kamel, 1998). Like the United States, South Africa has an ambivalent attitude toward corporal punishment; it continues to be practiced despite a variety of prohibitions and limitations on its use. In a paper presented at the annual meeting of the National Organization on Legal Problems in Education, J. Prinsloo (1994) described the problem of corporal punishment in South Africa and how it was allowed to be inflicted on students under South African common law. But less than 3 years after that presentation, on January 1, 1997, corporal punishment on any learner was banned, whether administered by a parent or a teacher within schools in South Africa (Foster, 1999, n.p.). The 1993 South African Constitution provides for fundamental rights for all South African citizens, yet a question remains as to whether the prohibition of cruel, inhuman, or degrading treatment or punishment (Section 11(2) of the Constitution) should apply to corporal punishment, in the face of parental opposition and, in some cases, parental support. In the United States, this issue, like all others related to education, is delegated to the individual states. The U.S. Supreme Court has ruled that, in itself, corporal punishment is not unconstitutional, as it does not meet the definition of "cruel and unusual punishment," which is prohibited by the Eighth Amendment to the U.S. Constitution. The Court has ruled that the cruel-and-unusual-punishment test applies to the treatment of incarcerated adults but, specifically, not to schoolchildren. This state sanctioning of corporal punishment in some U.S. localities has prompted concerned parents to remove their children from public schools and provide schooling for their children at home.

Oppressive school environments may include harsh authoritarian policies (like the condoning of strip searches), yet school can also feel oppressive because of student-to-student antisocial behaviors, which typically flourish in a permissive environment in which adult leadership is weak (or absent, as in Golding's novel *Lord of the Flies*). Whether oppressive environments are permissive or authoritarian, either will have detrimental effects on students, who become less able to focus on academics. Students in either environment may also be those students at highest risk for antisocial behavior, either as an initiator or as a victim or as both victim and initiator in turn. This idea takes on ominous implications when we look at the trend toward urbanization and the trend toward larger, urban schools, which are increasingly perceived as unsafe places and show a concomitant elevation in crime rates. In the United States, serious crimes, including rape, robbery, and physical attacks with or without a weapon, are 3 times more likely to occur in larger schools (enrollment over 1,000 students) than in smaller schools. This is true even when the number of crimes is calculated on a per-student basis (U.S. Department of Education, 1998).

Recent information on crime and violence in South Africa reveals that the nation's crime rate is high—perhaps twice the world average—with the incidence of serious crimes like murder and rape ranking South Africa's rates among the highest in the world (South Africa Online, 1999). According to the South African Police Service's (2000) *Bulletin on Reported Crime,* several crimes have been on the increase in South Africa (including serious assault, residential housebreaking, and robbery), while the rates of reported rape (41 crimes per 100,000 population) and murder (15.1 crimes per 100,000 population) remain high but seem to have leveled off in 2000. Nonetheless, in its most recent travel advisory, the U.S. Consular Service (U.S. Department of State, 1999b) warned that "Crime in South Africa is perceived to be a significant threat to the country's overall stability and to the welfare of its citizens" (n.p.), and the Service issued cautions for Americans traveling to South Africa.

In South African schools, children generally face violence from a number of sources, including violence from other students, and violence from teachers themselves (including teachers ignoring antisocial behavior and violence that is child-to-child). Corporal punishment is still carried out in some South African schools, even though it was banned throughout the nation in 1997 and despite the fact that the ban was recently upheld by the Eastern Cape High Court (Foster, 1999). But this ban has not been unchallenged, as members of Christian Education South Africa (CESA) are appealing the decision of the High Court, alleging it infringes on their religious beliefs and contradicts the wishes of parents. "Basically, what we've said to our schools is that they need to establish what the parents believe on the issue," said Ian Vermooten, executive director of CESA. In the meantime, Foster (1999) adds, "many of the 209 [CESA] member schools will continue to beat children" (n.p.).

Corporal punishment continues at rural schools in South Africa's Northern Province, which has prompted the South African Human Rights Commission (SAHRC) to introduce a series of debates on the issue. Provincial SAHRC coordinator Ntshole Mabapa said that the debates would involve 14 township and rural schools. "The intention is to get the schools to come up with ideas to instill discipline instead of resorting to corporal punishment," which Mabapa claimed was not as prevalent in the schools of South Africa's towns and cities. The debates are organized in conjunction with the South African Council of Churches, which began training volunteers in early 2000 to help impart management skills to the most difficult schools in the province (Hammond, 2000, n.p.).

In addition to corporal punishment, children also face threats to their safety in areas such as sexual abuse by adults and by other students. In response to recent concerns about sexual abuse, South African Minister of Education Kader Asmal pledged to root out sexual violence in schools. Writing for the *Daily Mail & Guardian,* Charlene Smith (1999) reported that, in response to the Minister's pledge, the Gauteng Department of Education had just completed training district officials, social workers, child-protection unit officers, and Department of Health officials in how to identify and address sexual abuse of children. Tinka Labuschagne, educational specialist with the Department of Education, said that the next stage will include training for school principals and teachers in identifying and dealing with sexual abuse of children (n.p.). Without question, children who are at risk of being beaten in school, or those who are forced to remain quiet in the face of abuse, are not children who feel safe.

These instances of physical abuse and punishment differ from what I observed in Finland and Russia. In my teaching visits to those nations in

1996 and 1998, I saw or heard of no instance of corporal punishment. Russian and Finnish teachers I interviewed seemed genuinely mystified by the idea that children should be beaten and were beaten by their school teachers. Several Finnish teachers answered my question about corporal punishment with the question, "Why would a teacher want to do that to a student?"

Schools as Safe Places

There is a correlation between the level of violence and safety in a culture and the level of violence and safety within the confines of schools within that culture. It is folly to suppose a violent culture or nation can have within its borders schools unaffected by the violence outside the school windows. Yet as stated previously, irrespective of the level of violence in the social context outside the school, children and adolescents tend to be safer in school than outside school. When one looks at the hazards children throughout the world confront—from illness and accidents either at home or while riding in a motor vehicle—one sees that school provides a relatively safe haven, particularly for children whose home and neighborhood are dangerous. Indeed, given the larger culture of antisocial behavior in America, it is truly amazing that schools have maintained such a high degree of relative safety under such circumstances. School is safe (or should be safe) because it provides a social milieu, a social circle and environment—physical and social—in which the child feels at home and can move and grow up (Prinsloo & Du Plessis, 1998, pp. 19-20). This social milieu is an essential socioeducative component of modern schools, and teachers form the heart of that milieu. Peace educator Ian Harris (2000) writes, "In this violent culture educators have a key role to play in teaching young people how to behave peacefully, in addressing the sources of violence in their lives and in helping them recover from violence" (p. 7).

Summary

Throughout the world, schools vary in the nature and quality of socialization provided to children and adolescents. In poorer nations, and in poorer states and regions within wealthy nations, schools typically reflect the problems and disadvantages that are part of their immediate context or neighborhood. In these poorer areas, schools seem to contribute to the problem of antisocial behavior by, for example, using corporal punishment as a way to settle conflict or deliver justice. Schools in poorer areas are reflective of the surrounding neighborhood and community. Although they can be relatively safe oases in violent neighborhoods, such schools are far from immune from the effects of outside violence and antisocial behavior. Schools in wealthier areas rarely use strong antiviolence measures. In the United States, it is safe to say that, irrespective of whether a state allows or prohibits corporal punishment, not one wealthy school district would use corporal punishment on a student. Like other types of violence, corporal punishment seems to go with the other effects of class and poverty. With about half of its people living in poverty, South Africa is the second most economically polarized country in the world (next to Brazil). Of those living in poverty are 60% of all South African children (Goodman, 1999, p. 17). Consequently, schools in poverty areas will be dramatically different—in the United States, Brazil, South Africa, and other nations—from schools in wealthier districts or regions. In fact, a ghetto school in Brazil will resemble a ghetto school in South Africa, Thailand, or the United States in more ways than it will resemble a wealthy school in Brazil. Conversely, wealthy schools will resemble other nations' wealthy schools more than they will resemble poorer schools within their own nation.

Nonetheless, schools throughout the world—rich or poor—are the most promising institutions society has to address some of the social problem areas in contemporary society. Of course, schools alone cannot reverse the effects of poverty and inequality, but they can serve as societies in microcosm and show us what can be. As a start, all schools—particularly schools in poverty areas—must move away from harsh or violent responses to antisocial behavior and violence, because antisocial behavior and violence are too readily learned. The most formidable obstacles faced in trying to maximize the potential of schools lies not only in the securing of adequate funding to maintain and improve those schools in poorer areas but also in the discovery of ways to ensure attendance by children in poverty. Simply being able to ensure attendance by children in schools that are adequately funded would be an important first step in bolstering the socialization role of public schools throughout the world, serving to move the school from being a problem to its being part of a solution.

Reframing Views on Antisocial Behavior

Best School Practices

In this age of emphasis on raising the bar on student achievement and raising standardized test scores, most Americans would be surprised to learn that, above all else, the American public wants its schools to teach social skills and to socialize America's young people. In a study by the National Center for Education Statistics and the Pelavin Research Institute, respondents in 12 industrialized nations were asked to rate the relative importance of educational subjects, character qualities (socialization skills), and employment-related skills. In the United States, academic subjects were rated important by 71% of those polled, and socialization skills were rated important by 85% of those polled (Galper, 1998). Internationally, social skills were consistently rated high, with the U.S. respondents pragmatically placing more emphasis on social skills leading to employability—being able to get a job—than other nations. American respondents recognized additional advantages of socialization, including advantages for society at large. These include quality-of-life issues, ranging from an avoidance of personal incarceration to an appreciation for democratic principles embodied in voting for candidates for public office.

Yet in light of this apparent public mandate for social skills and socialization, schools today appear to be underachieving or failing. Having been asked to respond to challenges of antisocial behavior and violence, schools have been given less than the best tools: medications and mind-numbing, ever-increasing compendia of laws, prohibitions, and mandates. These do little toward enabling schools to do what they can do best: teach social skills, attitudes, and concepts to young people. In the ongoing national concern about antisocial behavior and violence, schools can help in a serious and effective way, perhaps more than any other social institution we have. However, schools must be allowed to do what they do best and not be forced to turn into quasi-prisons or rehabilitation centers. For example, emphasis on zero-tolerance responses to rule infractions has moved attention away from what prosocial behaviors students should learn and toward what punishments will be brought to bear. Suspension, detention, and expulsion are unproductive, exacerbating responses to a serious social problem. Researchers Skiba and Peterson (1999b) reported that schools with zero-tolerance policies for violence were more likely than schools with no zero-tolerance policy to have reported serious crime. This is not surprising, because schools with more crime might be more likely to enact such policies. Yet 4 years after zero-tolerance policies were implemented, schools with zero-tolerance policies in place were still less safe; no measurable effect has been seen that can be attributed to zero-tolerance policies. In addition, it must be remembered that students who are outside of school are far more likely to commit a crime, to use drugs, and to engage in antisocial behavior than students who are enrolled in school and those who are actively attending school.

Aside from policies, security hardware is also of dubious benefit. Visible trappings of school security, such as guards, checkpoints, handprint readers, metal detectors, and video cameras are of unproven worth: There is simply no evidence that visible security hardware or personnel have any impact on reducing antisocial or violent student behavior. These measures may paradoxically increase alienation among students who are cynically resentful of what one student told me were "Rent-a-Cops" in his school cafeteria. Similarly, medicating children may serve to placate some parents and teachers, but there is no evidence that these medical measures are safe over a long term, and there is no evidence that student behavior is significantly improved in any long-term or socially productive way, even when students regularly take their prescribed medication.

On the Role of Schools in Socialization

Parents, family, and peers as well as schools all play a highly influential role in socializing children toward prosocial and antisocial behaviors. It may be safe to say that, as an agent of socialization, today's schools play an even greater role than ever before. Some have claimed that schools have "become the primary instrument of socialization" (Siegel & Senna, 1997, p. 361) and "the basic conduit" through which adult and community influences reach the young person (Polk & Schaefer, 1972, p. 13). Teachers are the linchpins in that socialization process, for it is they who are closest to students and have the potential to make a difference in a student's life more than any other professional. In *Positive Classroom Management,* I (2000) wrote,

> Except for a few social workers and trial lawyers, today's teachers are the only professionals our society has—and will likely have in the future—who stand between a student and jail. If students fail to learn prosocial behavior, their misbehavior and antisocial behavior soon become matters for the legal system and, ultimately, prison. (p. 6)

Jane Roland Martin (1992), author of *The Schoolhome,* believes that because society is so different today from in the past, our schools must emphasize socialization. They must teach both the basics—the three Rs and the three Cs (care, concern, and connection). Martin acknowledges the importance of students' vocational needs, but she also stresses that we need to prepare students—men and women—for the *reproductive* aspects of society, including caring for other people, raising children, and sustaining a home. Martin argues that we should come to see the school as a *schoolhome,* something more than the traditional schoolhouse. In many ways, schools have already moved in that direction by providing lunch programs, health care, and extended day care in some places. But this should be extended to include a domestic curriculum as part of the school's very fabric, which would serve to complement parental roles as well as emphasize prosocial behavior.

School-Related Violence That Cannot Be Predicted

Identifying school-related factors that contribute to or foster antisocial behavior and violence has been relatively difficult to accomplish, mostly due to the complexity of the social environment of the school. G. R. Mayer (1995) acknowledges the difficulty in isolating and identifying contributors to antisocial behavior, attributing the main problem to the existence of "setting events" that occur in school environments. Setting events are incidents or "antecedents that may occur within the same setting and closely precede the antisocial behavior," such as a child being poked by another as the teacher addresses the child, or the student having just argued with another during recess (p. 470). Sometimes, the effects of setting events can be cumulative, and "several instructions followed by several errors can serve as a setting event for the next instruction occasioning problem behavior such as aggression" (Munk & Repp, 1994, p. 391).

To further complicate the question of causality, some serious forms of violence cannot be anticipated or predicted, and some of it, perhaps, will never be understood. Celeste Kennel-Shank (2000) wrote that

> in truth, there will never be any reason—whether it is television, video games, bad parenting, a secular society, or the press itself— that fully explains how an adolescent, even (a child) as young as 9 years old, can murder his or her classmates and teachers and feel a surge of power at watching them die. (p. 49)

When we speak of tragic and horrible events, such as the murderous acts at Columbine High School in 1999 or the shooting of a first-grade Michigan student and a Florida teacher in 2000, we will never fully comprehend the reasons for such events. Accordingly, it is likely that such disasters may never be completely predictable or, as a result, preventable. But this sobering thought should never turn us away from actively working to prevent violence that can be predicted and thus prevented, and it should not drive us to take desperate measures.

School-Related Violence That Can Be Predicted

Although some antisocial behavior cannot be predicted or anticipated, it is clear that some forms of violent behavior, such as fist fights between students or physical aggression by a student directed at a teacher, have identifiable antecedents or forewarnings. Those who have studied the origins of interpersonal violence describe the existence of triggers that set into motion events leading up to interpersonal violence. In an analysis of violence among middle school and high school students who attended public schools at which the level of violence is high, criminal-justice professor Daniel Lockwood (1997), writing for the National Institute of Justice, studied violence and aggression among middle school and high school students. He found that in most violent incidents, there was an "opening move" that consisted of "a relatively minor affront but escalated from there." Lockwood also found that "the most common goal" that underpinned these affronts was a sense of retribution. He found that students who initiated violence did not lack values, but actually had "a well-developed value system in which violence is acceptable" (p. 2). This sense of retribution is the seed from which much antisocial behavior and violence grows and may be what lies behind road rage and other shockingly strong acts of antisocial behavior. Kauffman and Burbach (1997) refer to this as " 'Slight Trigger Disease,' an impulsive response to anything that can be construed as offensive" (p. 321), and it appears that much can be construed as an offense. When students explained the reasons for their violent behaviors, the majority (84%) of aggressors in Lockwood's (1997) study accepted responsibility for their actions but denied that these actions were wrong. "Their actions were bolstered by a strong belief system, evident in these justifications, which served to neutralize any guilt" (p. 2).

Is violence predictable? Some authors suggest that the human propensity toward violent behavior grows from lesser antisocial behavior, including arguments and disagreements over what appear to be trivial matters. Violent behavior may appear to arise suddenly, but in fact violent behavior is a result of lower-level aggressive behavior that grows increasingly violent in stages or steps. In *Violence and Aggression in Children and Youth,* written for the U.S. Department of Education, Mary K. Fitzsimmons (1998) highlighted five stages of frustration in which students who engage in antisocial behavior show behavior that grows progressively more forceful, leading to violence. The stages include

1. *Anxiety.* The student will sigh or use other nonverbal cues. This is the lowest level of aggression, which is behavior that is not clearly antisocial, although it is the starting point of antisocial behavior.

2. *Stress.* The student will show minor behavior problems.

3. *Defensiveness.* The student will argue and complain. This will usually occur in reaction to a teacher's intervention or attempt to intervene in the student's antisocial behavior.

4. *Physical Aggression or Violence.* At this point of escalation, the student may hit, kick, bite, or throw objects. Here, teachers' first priority is to protect the safety of the student, the safety of other students, and their own safety. The student is usually escorted out of the room, and the teacher usually seeks the help of other adults.

5. *Tension Reduction.* This is a denouement in which the student releases tension through crying or verbal venting, or the student might remain quiet and withdrawn (p. 2).

In his important book *Solving Discipline Problems,* Charles Wolfgang (1995, pp. 286-287) describes four levels of crisis development that lead up to possible violent student behavior. At each level, Wolfgang provides practical goals and techniques for teachers to use to recognize and deal with students at each of the four levels. The first level is potential crisis—attention getting, where the student is like a tightly wound spring. The students may clench their hands; they may focus their sights directly on the teacher or other student, and they may show other signs of nervousness, such as pacing or facial tics. The teacher seeks to engage an angry student verbally, to talk it out, allowing the student to ventilate through language.

Level two involves a developing crisis—power, through which the student shows defiance, consisting of verbal outbursts, swearing, screaming, or shouting. These may appear to be ventilation of stored-up tension. At this stage, the teacher uses an "alert supportive stance," permitting "the child's ventilation through verbal aggression." The teacher may also need to provide "an assertive command" (p. 278) and promise safety to the student at the same time. This stage may escalate into level three, imminent crisis—assault/revengeful, where angry students become fully irrational and lose control of their actions. They physically strike out against another by choking, biting, hitting, or throwing. In response, teachers defend themselves, using restraining techniques combined with an assertive command telling the student to desist action and reassuring the student of safety.

The last level is level four, reestablishing equilibrium. The student is now deflated and has become passive and lethargic. At this point, the teacher's role is to help the student recapitulate what happened, first by having the student talk about it, then by attempting to reestablish the relationship verbally, and by touch. An understanding of these levels of crisis are probably unknown to most teachers, despite their vital importance in predicting and preventing (or at least, limiting) potentially violent behavior.

Unfortunately, little or no instruction is available to teachers or student teachers on the use of preventive techniques, such as Fitzsimmons's stages or Wolfgang's levels of crisis development. It is as if educators are simply hoping for the best, waiting for something to happen that we hope won't happen before we are forced to react.

School Contexts and Antisocial Behavior

There are other ways that antisocial and violent behavior can be prevented. Recently, school researchers have looked at the connection between the type of physical environment of the school building and student antisocial and violent behavior. They have found that within different areas within each school, the degree of safety, both actual and perceived, varies more than had been suspected. There are what researchers called *owned* and *unowned* spaces in U.S. high schools, and it is precisely within the unowned spaces that antisocial behavior and violence is more likely to occur. These spaces are called unowned because teachers do not tend to see them as their area of responsibility (in contrast to classrooms, which are owned in teachers' and students' eyes). Students see unowned places as places that belong neither to teachers nor to students. Unowned high school spaces include school hallways, cafeterias, bathrooms, and outside grounds. Looking at five American high schools, researchers Astor, Meyer, and Behre (1999) found that in the schools they examined, violent behaviors occurred exclusively in unowned spaces. This finding is especially relevant to those who educate younger children, who may feel less safe from antisocial behavior than adolescents or adults. Younger adolescent students (12 and 13 years of age), are more likely to be victimized by antisocial behavior than younger children or even young adults (Stein & Mulrine, 1999), and it is likely that owned and unowned places in school loom large in their feelings of safety.

There are unowned times as well as unowned spaces in school. These are times within the school day when antisocial behavior and violence are likely to occur. Typically, these times are at the beginning and end of school and during transition times, such as on the way to activities and during lunch or study hall (free time). In Russia in 1996 and 1998, I observed all-too-familiar student behaviors regarding owned and unowned spaces and times in two rural comprehensive schools (elementary through high school grades). Outside each school building, I saw several young, preadolescent male students huddled in groups of three or four, drinking alcoholic beverages and smoking cigarettes, outside the eye of any teacher and at transition times between classes when their absence from the school was not likely to be noticed. They engaged in these behaviors near or behind the school building, just outside of main traffic areas. On the other hand, we visiting American and Canadian educators were impressed by the clear ownership of classrooms within the school by Russian teachers and students, and we witnessed genuine courtesy and respect accorded teachers by Russian students. This respect was returned in teachers' behavior toward students.

In addition to the effects of the physical context of the school, the connection between the social context and antisocial behavior has also been studied. As mentioned earlier, although it is difficult to pinpoint social factors that bring about antisocial behavior, researchers have used correlational analyses to recognize situations and teacher behaviors that appear to be related to student antisocial behavior. Researcher G. R. Mayer (1995) has found three social-context factors that appear to be related to student antisocial behavior: clarity, support for teaching staff, and allowance for student differences.

Clarity. A lack of clarity correlates with antisocial behavior. Students whose behavior is antisocial tend to lack a clear understanding of general classroom policies as well as specific rules and expectations for behavior. Teachers who are not clear with students also experience a greater degree of classroom management problems. This can result in a vicious cycle of sorts, in which the teacher will respond with corrective, after-the-fact interventions that may be punitive or harsh, to which the student may respond with further antisocial behavior. It is interesting to point out that, in addition to its influence on student behavior, clarity in teaching also improves student achievement (Dunkin & Barnes, 1986, p. 766).

It makes sense to assume that teachers who can convey clear expectations, as well as those teachers who clarify roles and behavioral expectations through class discussions, will be more effective in managing group behavior. It helps students when their teachers believe that they—the teachers—can have a positive and clear impact on students. Conversely, it helps students when students believe that they can have a positive impact on what happens in their classroom, on themselves, and on other students (self-efficacy).

Administrative Support. Mayer found that support of staff shows an inverse correlation with student antisocial behavior: The greater the support given to staff, the less antisocial behavior is seen in students. Conversely, the incidence of antisocial behavior increases when administrative support is lacking or is weak or inconsistent and when there is an absence of administrative follow-through. Lack of administrative support results in fairly predictable types of disruptions of continuity between teacher and students. For example, teacher absenteeism tends to be higher in situations in which there is less administrative support (Manlove & Elliott, 1979; Spuck, 1974). Two studies looked at the connection between student vandalism and administrative support for teachers, and they found that when administrative support was absent or inconsistent, teachers were more likely to rely on punitive methods of managing students (Mayer, Butterworth, Komoto, & Benoit, 1983; Mayer & Sulzer-Azaroff, 1991). Mayer (1995) adds that inconsistent behavior on the part of the school administration "appears to result in inconsistent follow-through by staff, often resulting in more behavior problems by students" (p. 471). This occurs when students perceive consequences to be unfairly applied, and when schools seem to favor some who receive preferential treatment.

This may be an especially relevant issue in some South African schools. In a recent examination of the role of black high school principals in South Africa, Gumbi (1995) found that there were many bureaucratic expectations that guided the principals' behavior. In addition, principals in Gumbi's study tended to work in violent school environments, disrupted by teacher and student strikes, to the point at which they were unable to provide leadership. As a starting point for South African school reform, Gumbi advocated the restoring of dignity to the role of the school principal, declaring the role to be pivotal in the new education transformation under South Africa's democratic government.

The role of the black school principal in the United States seems to have suffered an earlier yet similar fate. Sociology professor Doris Wilkinson (1999) described how harmful the 1954 *Brown versus Topeka Board of Education* U.S. Supreme Court decision was for black Americans despite its reputation as a landmark in civil rights for American blacks. As a result of that court decision, "many schools designed for African American children were closed" (p. 129), with black children sent from schools that honored their black heroes to schools that were predominantly white, depriving black children of their historical and cultural roots and depriving them of the rich support of the black community schools. Wilkinson added that black teachers were gradually transferred away from their community schools or they were fired, but even more damaging was the outcome that "the African American principal—often a male hero and community leader—became obsolete. The loss of this black role model and parental figure has had far-reaching ramifications" (p. 129). Although the Supreme Court decision was legally correct, its social repercussions were highly disruptive to a stable black community and its social order.

Allowing for Student Differences. Students come to school with a variety of academic strengths and a variety of social skills. It is, perhaps, obvious to point out that students who have poor academic skills and poor achievement are those more likely to engage in antisocial behavior in school. Center, Deitz, and Kaufman (1982) said that "failure level academic tasks resulted in significant increases in inappropriate behavior in some students" (p. 355). Failure in academic work sets the stage for antisocial behavior, and the teacher's ability to consider and respond to the needs of students to be successful is quite critical in moderating antisocial behavior. The teachers' task is particularly difficult when their students have experienced failure in school and have become accustomed to it as a way of life. With such students, there is no quick fix or easy path to success. Harsh and punitive responses by the teacher serve to maintain (and confirm) student antisocial behavior. A recognition of student differences implies that the teacher recognizes (and searches for) qualities in each student that are strengths or possible areas for success. This involves more than giving praise and rewards to students.

Following several qualitative studies involving surveys, interviews, and observations of teachers, I came up with three axioms that highlight the connection between students' academic success and prosocial behavior (DiGiulio, 2000, pp. 47-49). The axioms hold that, first, students who feel successful in school seldom present behavior problems. Second, to feel successful in schoolwork, students must actually *be* successful—praise and rewards by themselves are insufficient. Third, to actually be successful, a student must first do something of value. Teachers should focus their first efforts on the third axiom by preparing and presenting activities and projects that allow different students—in different ways—to experience real success. All too often, schoolwork consists of a narrow band of norm-referenced activities (reading, writing, calculating, etc.) that are designed so that only some students will do well at these tasks, and even fewer will do extremely well. For the less successful remainder of the students, these activities represent tests of their ability, interest, and patience, tests that seem to produce failure time and again. Consequently, these less successful students are more likely to misbehave, act out, and engage in antisocial behavior. Conversely, they are also the ones who stand to profit most from a teacher who is attuned to their different abilities and strengths. For example, there are teachers who use a teaching format that allows students to use their strengths. Howard Gardner's multiple intelligences theory comes to mind as an example of an organizing framework that recognizes different strengths or intelligences within each student. Teachers can then teach to those strengths and enable students to use their strong areas to learn in areas in which they are less capable. Students at risk for antisocial behavior are also those most likely to profit from a teacher who can proactively teach them social skills that would reduce or eliminate their antisocial behaviors that serve to provoke or harm others. Such students are not helped by laissez-faire teachers who provide little or no structure, and students are not helped by teachers who emphasize punishment, because there is little constructive or instructive in being beaten or humiliated. Threats and harsh punishments are counterproductive—diametrically opposed to helping students be successful. Ironically, it is the students from violent homes who are most in need of clear, caring, and strong teacher support, in the interest of their being successful in school.

Best School-Level Preventive Responses to Antisocial Behavior: Physical, Programmatic, and Personnel Responses

Best Physical Responses

Shrink huge schools. Long before he ran for president, H. Ross Perot said the reason Texas had so many huge high schools was that greater size increased a high school's chances of fielding the tallest and heaviest—and thus most successful—football team. Although he meant his comment as a humorous aside, there is much to question about the advantages provided by huge, warehouse high schools, those that house 2,000 or 3,000 students. Raywid and Oshiyama (2000) wrote, "There is overwhelming evidence that violence is much less likely to occur in small schools than in large ones" (p. 445). Indeed, one clear finding in the recent U.S. Department of Education (1998) report on *Violence and Discipline in the U.S.*

Public Schools was that larger schools—those with enrollments of 1,000 students or more—were 8 times more likely than smaller schools to report at least one serious violent crime. Large schools breed anonymity, which results in separation and alienation. James Garbarino, codirector of the Family Life Development Center at Cornell University, was recently quoted as saying that if he could do one thing to stop juvenile violence, "it would be to ensure that teenagers are not in high schools bigger than 400 to 500 students" (Gladden, 1998, p. 116).

There are additional advantages to smaller schools. Columbia University Teachers College Professor Linda Darling-Hammond (1995) summarized numerous research, including her own investigations, and she concluded that

> smaller schools and school units . . . are associated with higher achievement, as well as better attendance rates, fewer dropouts, and lower levels of students misbehavior. They are more effective in allowing students to become bonded to important adults in a learning community, who can play the role that families and communities find it harder and harder to play. They are also more effective in creating good interpersonal relationships, and in providing opportunities for students to participate in extracurricular activities and to take leadership roles. (p. 155)

Revise school design. In addition to building smaller schools, we need to build into those smaller schools smaller, more intimate spaces that lend themselves to people being relatively close together (but not crowded in together). There is not only a social benefit but also an academic benefit: The physical arrangement within the classroom has an effect on student academic performance and behavior (Doyle, 1986). High student density is a problem associated with increased aggression, inattentiveness, and distractibility among students (Keogh, 1998). These problems seem to be most severe for students with low abilities.

Planners and designers of schools must eliminate remote, hard-to-own places within schools and seek to arrange spaces within schools that can be owned. This involves an assessment of distance from other student areas as well as of lighting and likely traffic patterns through and near each area. Hours of operation may also be a factor: Some school boards have changed the hours of the high school day, starting school later (9:00 a.m. or 9:30 a.m.), allowing students to get additional sleep. Although there is little research on the efficacy of such a measure, some anecdotal information indicates that students are better able to learn when they are well rested.

Best Programmatic Responses

Adopt in-school programs that work. There have been many violence-prevention programs designed for use in schools. Early reviews of the usefulness of these programs were mixed. Few programs resulted in a reduction of violence. Daniel Webster (1993) looked at three early efforts at violence-prevention curricula and found there was no evidence of a long-term change in violent behavior.

However, more recently devised violence-prevention programs appear to work well and hold more promise. In a 16-month evaluation sponsored by the National Institute of Justice, Project S.T.O.P (Schools Teaching Options for Peace), and the Safe Harbor Program, two violence-prevention programs used in the New York public school system appeared to produce positive results (U.S. Department of Justice, 1995). Project S.T.O.P was a conflict-resolution program that included both a conflict-resolution curriculum and a peer-mediator component; the Safe Harbor Program included a 20-session curriculum, a counseling component, and a whole-school antiviolence curriculum. Evaluations of both programs after extensive use in four middle schools showed four significant results. First, and as may have been expected, students who had been victimized in the past were more likely than nonvictimized students to participate in one or both programs. Second, students who participated in the Safe Harbor Program were less likely to advocate retaliation in response to conflict than students who had not participated in the program. Third, students who participated in Project S.T.O.P. showed a reduction in feelings of helplessness. Last, and perhaps most valuable, it was found that students who participated in both programs also altered their prior belief that respect was achieved through violence.

Programmatic efforts have also been directed toward altering the overall school environment in preventing violent and antisocial behavior. Programs such as PeaceBuilders emphasize a holistic, schoolwide approach (Noddings, 1996) that teaches through adult modeling both in the day-to-day interactions and throughout instruction in each regular curricular content area. The program emphasizes five principles for students including praising of others, avoiding put-downs, seeking wise people as advisors and friends, noticing and correcting the hurts one may have caused, and right-ing any wrongs (Schwartz, 1999, pp. 1-9). Resolving Conflict Creatively (RCCP) seeks to transform an entire school culture to one of nonviolence (Pont-Brown & Krumboltz, 1999, p. 50). Created by Linda Lantieri in 1985, RCCP teaches students to use nonviolent conflict-resolution measures, such as listening to each other when a dispute arises, in order to work toward a peaceful solution. The program has been successful in increasing students' conflict-resolution skills as well as reducing physical violence in the classroom and reducing insults and verbal put-downs (Lantieri, 1995).

Both the RCCP and the Peacemakers Program (which was successfully implemented in the Cleveland Public School system) take a combined classroom-based and schoolwide approach toward infusing a nonviolence ethic throughout the school culture. The Peacemakers Program reduced aggression-related disciplinary incidents by 41%, accompanied by a 67% decrease in violent-behavior-related school suspensions (Shapiro, 1999).

Educators in Oregon have developed a schoolwide approach to discipline called *effective behavior support,* which also emphasizes prevention. Researchers at the University of Oregon teamed up with public school administrators and teachers to implement this program that teaches students appropriate conduct. Teachers within a school agree on three to five overall goals, then teachers work together to instruct students in appropriate actions to attain those goals. The program has been successful in over 300 schools in Oregon, Hawaii, Illinois, and British Columbia, with reductions in office referrals, improved school climate, and the reduction of placements in special education for some students. The program's methods, according to Professor Robert Horner of the University of Oregon, "are a direct rebuttal to lawmakers' 'get tough' stands on discipline, including measures in Congress to give administrators greater power to suspend or expel" (Sack, 1999, pp. 32-33). The heart of the approach involves directly teaching students expected behavior, modeling expected behavior, and reminding students about appropriate behavior. "Before recess, for instance, Patterson Elementary teachers talk to their students about appropriate behavior on the playground" (p. 33), and the entire school works together with this preventive goal as its shared first priority. Ms. Jackson would fully agree.

Establish after-school and summer programs. Professor and peace educator Ian Harris cofounded a week-long Summer Institute at the University of Wisconsin—Milwaukee campus that taught nonviolence to young adolescents 13 to 15 years of age. By its scope and its emphasis on best practices, the Institute provided an innovative and constructive response to adolescent violence. It combined peace education curricula with an emphasis on creating and maintaining supportive social networks, and it stressed the power of nonviolence. In Harris's (1999) words, "The best way to build peaceful behavior in our youth is to convince young people to value peace" (p. 325). Ultimately, holistic approaches that seek to reduce or eliminate student antisocial behavior must introduce and maintain what Hawkins, Farrington, and Catalano (1998) refer to as the *norm of nonviolence* within the school. This includes the setting of a calm and predictable atmosphere that fosters a sense of security, limiting the power of unseen events to launch explosive behavior (Schwartz, 1999, p. 5). Harris's program has served as a model for other peace education efforts.

Even programs not specifically geared to peace education can be immensely important to socialization. Prior to New York City's first financial crisis in the mid-1970s, two successful programs kept thousands of mostly poor, mostly working-class youngsters off the streets and engaged in constructive activity. As a teacher in the city's VDC (Vacation Day Camp) and ECC (Evening Community Center) programs, I saw first-hand that by opening the schools to young people during the summer and until nine o'clock in the evening throughout the rest of the year, and by providing competent supervision within those programs, young persons were productively occupied with sports, games, music, drama, and crafts. Unfortunately, these New York City Board of Education community education programs were early casualties of a fiscal crisis that, by 1976, would also force the layoff of hundreds of regular New York City classroom teachers.

Sponsor school-based parent education. Agencies such as Oregon's Social Learning Center provide parent education through programs such as its Parent Management Training, in which parents learn how to be in charge of children without using harsh punishments or humiliation. Parents are taught how to set clear limits and how to avoid power struggles. Some children, unfortunately, are so out of control and have suffered such profound abuse that they must be removed from their homes. For these extreme cases, the Center houses a unique Treatment Foster Care Program that recruits and trains special foster parents for each child. Attracted to the Center through newspaper advertisements, these made-to-order parents are paid well to serve as a surrogate family for each child with severe behavior problems. The key element in the Center's success with this latter program is that "children and adolescents are kept away from other troubled children and adolescents," according to Patricia Chamberlain, program director (Storring & Zaritsky, 2000, n.p.); and they are integrated into a normal, healthy home environment. Research has shown that when children are in traditional foster care, both the severity and frequency of violent behavior increase greatly in children as young as 6 years of age. The Treatment Foster Care Program has shown a marked decrease in arrests: In a 5-year study, 79 adolescent boys with a criminal record were randomly assigned to either a traditional foster-care group home or the Oregon Center's Treatment Foster Care for up to 9 months. One year following the end of treatment, the boys in traditional foster homes had an average of 5.4 arrests, and those in Treatment Foster Care showed 2.6 arrests. Chamberlain attributed the difference to "increased adult supervision and decreased contact with other 'deviant' peers" (n.p.).

In sum, schools work well as resources for parents, and when the two parties work together, it is to the benefit of the children and adolescents. For instance, schools have provided much help to parents when there is bullying behavior, help for both the parents of the children doing the bullying, and for the students who are victims (Banks, 1997). Programs such as Linking the Interests of Families and Teachers (LINK) have also been successful but only when such programs take a more comprehensive approach, particularly in neighborhoods that have high levels of unemployment, gang membership, divorce, domestic abuse, and violence. Given that schools are relatively safe places for children, extending that safety to parents (by inviting them into school and by providing resources in school for the parents) can make a big difference in such seemingly hopeless circumstances.

Increase early intervention into aggressive behavior. As mentioned earlier, aggressive and antisocial behavior at an early age is quite durable; it predicts the likelihood of more serious behavior and criminal behavior later in adolescence and young adulthood. It is thus imperative that efforts are made to identify best practices for parents, day care workers, and preschool teachers that can be translated big into workable ways to stop antisocial behavior in young children. What parenting practices are effective with the aggressive youngster? What do successful preschool teachers do when faced with aggressive behavior? There is a lot of anecdotal material but relatively little clear information about those crucially important questions.

Train personal-behavior coaches. Just as the Treatment Foster Care Program attracts made-to-order foster parents for students who have exhibited violent behavior, perhaps we can attract the best teachers to serve as one-to-one models, *designer teachers* for youngsters. Such a plan would require funding, as the youngsters it would serve would probably have few financial resources to pay for such services. Teachers would act in ways similar to traditional Big Brother and Big Sister programs' volunteers: Like adult mentors, teachers would be matched with young people at risk.

Best Personnel Responses

Of the three areas of response (physical, programmatic, and personnel), personnel responses hold the most potential to change antisocial behavior. More important than the physical design or size of the school, and at the heart of any quality programs and curricula that are being implemented, lies the person-to-person relationship between teacher and student. Studies of school violence have shown that matters most under the potential control of the teacher (levels of student achievement as well as classroom and school atmosphere) play a key role in reducing school violence (Howard, 1981; Zwier & Vaughan, 1984). Teachers who work to increase students' academic success, for example, will not automatically eliminate student antisocial behavior, but they will be reducing the opportunities for antisocial behavior to occur. When a student is successful in academic work, it is less likely that he or she will present a behavior problem. As a result, teachers who work toward building and maintaining student success have fewer discipline problems, because the motivation they provide is the best of all types: It is intrinsic motivation. All students want and need to do well, and all students want and need to be recognized as being good at or in something, far more than they need rewards or hollow praise.

Emphasize caring interventions. As a prerequisite for this intrinsic motivation, students must fundamentally believe that teachers care about them. There are many ways that teachers can convey this message. Caring is shown by ways so obvious that they are being taken for granted: by involving students in the discussion of classroom procedures, by creating constructivist learning opportunities, by looking at students when talking to them, by being genuinely interested in students, and by welcoming students to participate as fully as possible in the life of the classroom. Aside from the good feelings that are aroused in a caring classroom, there is one additional social outcome of teacher caring: Over time, student prosocial behavior graduates; it becomes *parent* prosocial behavior, *lover* prosocial behavior, *spouse* prosocial behavior, and so on.

Antirewards crusader Alfie Kohn (1993) emphasizes that "it is not a matter of what the teacher does for (or, better, with) this child and that one but rather how a caring classroom and school community can be created to serve as the context in which children acquire positive attitudes and skills" (p. 246). The main job falls on the teacher to support this school-home concept. It is imperative, therefore, that each teacher receive support from parents, community, and school administration toward this challenging yet vital task.

Russell J. Quaglia (2000), director of the National Center for Student Aspirations, cites his organization's recent survey of over 50,000 students across the United States. "More than 90% said they believed teachers are concerned about their academic growth, but only 40% believe their teachers care about their personal and social problems or their feelings" (p. 56). Other research has pointed to caring interventions by teachers as an extremely essential—perhaps, the most essential—in-school component in the prevention of antisocial and violent behavior. Recently, researchers identified schools in neighborhoods with high rates of juvenile crime. The researchers recruited the families of every first- and fifth-grade student and paid schools and teachers to hold sessions teaching children how to solve problems and how to play in nonaggressive ways. Playground monitors "stopped kids from hassling one another," said John Reid, cofounder of the Social Learning Center, who added that "even real tough kids don't like to bully other kids in front of adults" (Storring & Zaritsky, 2000). Two and a half years after the experiment ended, Reid continued to interview the students and observe signs of success. He found that playground fights and antisocial behavior decreased in the presence of active adult deterrence, a finding that is especially encouraging in light of the fact that the children were now young adolescents and thus at an age of higher risk for antisocial behavior as well as arrest for juvenile crime.

Indeed, other research upholds not only the value of each act of intervention but also the quality of each intervention.

Consistent exposure to caring adult behavior results in empathetic child behavior—behavior that is more concerned with others' feelings and rights (Lipscomb, MacAllister, & Bregman, 1985). Researchers Astor, Meyer, and Behre (1999) noted a striking connection between high-quality, caring behaviors by teachers, and nonviolent student behavior in school. They identified teachers who "made efforts to ensure students' attendance, expected students to do quality work, and went beyond what the students expected in terms of personal support." Such teachers, who were perceived as most caring, responded clearly and unequivocally to potential violence. "These teachers claimed that they would intervene regardless of location and time." They did not perceive hallways and other undefined spaces in schools as unowned, but felt they owned the whole school territory or whatever space the student occupied, expressing that they felt personally obligated "to the whole child regardless of the setting, location, time, or expected professional role" (p. 24). These teachers saw their behaviors as similar to those of good parents. It is interesting to add that, although school administrators admired these teachers, they were not necessarily offered overt or formal support. They acted alone and oftentimes courageously. Other teachers expressed an interest in increasing their caring involvement but were hesitant to do so without more support from the administration. Among this latter group of teachers, the researchers noted "a pervasive sense of powerlessness regarding what they could and couldn't do" (p. 25). Whereas some teachers could respond strongly and in a caring way to students, it appears that many more need support from the school administration and other faculty before they can do so.

Interestingly, the movies *Blackboard Jungle* and *Stand and Deliver* fairly accurately portray teachers who do not accept their students' antisocial behavior, and neither teacher turns his back on students who are either perpetrators or victims of antisocial behavior. Both films provide excellent examples of caring interventions by teachers, both of whom work with minimal support from outside their classrooms.

Re-empower teachers. Educator Martin Haberman (1997) describes the situation in contemporary urban schools not as teaching and learning but as a "socialization battle." He asks if urban educators will be able to socialize their students to the work and adult worlds, or will students socialize their educators into their street values? "Currently," Haberman writes, "there is no contest. Urban youngsters and their street values are clearly the dominant force," supporting the ideology of poverty instead of values that lead to success in society (p. 503). Other educators agree that teachers must take back the school from groups of students who are calling the shots. Haberman points out that even in schools where educators still control the school environment, students receive no systematic training on violence alternatives. There is some evidence that students believe that adults don't know how to intervene, are afraid to intervene, or are unwilling to do so. In one study, students characterized adult intervention as "infrequent and ineffective" (Banks, 1997, n.p.), whereas Canadian researchers found that students say teachers seldom or never talk to their students in class about bullying (Charach, Pepler, & Zeigler, 1995). Other teachers may simply believe that it is important for students to work things out by themselves without relying on adult intervention. At its extreme, this laissez-faire strategy is probably the most effective way to perpetuate student bullying behavior. In all cases, the deterrence provided by adult or teacher intervention is vital, particularly in situations of student-to-student power imbalances, such as bully-victim situations. Yet to effectively intervene, teachers must themselves be empowered to do so. This empowerment of teachers is essential not because teachers must control students and deliver punishing consequences but so that teachers are able to set up and carry out a program that will create a safe in-school context and, ultimately, aid all students to move away from violent behavior. *This cannot be done with the teacher in an intimidated, passive, or weakened position or through laissez-faire classroom management.*

A sense of powerlessness may be even stronger among teachers working in poorer, more challenging schools and communities throughout the world. Powerlessness will impair a teacher's predisposition toward making caring interventions, increasing the likelihood that interventions may be strained, angry, harsh, and abusive. In her study of teacher education in South Africa's Northern Province, C. S. Mamabolo (1997) acknowledged the relatively low status of teachers, and she advocated improved inservice education. In a comparison of South African and U.S. teachers' participation in decision making, Magau (1999) noted many similarities, yet found that the South African teachers seemed particularly concerned about deteriorating school facilities, low teacher morale, uncertainty surrounding the rapid transitions in South African society, as well as the powerlessness they felt in dealing with a bureaucratic educational tradition. Richard Curwin (1995), author of *Discipline With Dignity,* writes that reducing violence in schools demands that teachers teach students alternatives to violence, and this implies the use of power in the welcoming of all students. Teacher power is best used not when reprimanding students but when we show them that we care about them and value them all equally. Unless we convey this, Curwin warns that "we will never extinguish the root causes of violence . . . and the false belief that stronger deterrents against a stereotyped them will make us safer" (p. 74).

It is essential to add that teachers and administrators alone cannot accomplish these measures without support from the political infrastructure. This major educational policy initiative would help greatly in strengthening the social narrative: Our children are important; our future is important. This initiative will certainly require greater monetary support for education. In a letter to the editor of *The New York Times,* M. Frank Phillips (2000), former president of the Great Neck [New York] Board of Education wrote,

> If lawmakers sincerely wish to give our disadvantaged children their human right to a good education, they will support legislation to pay for enrolling all 3-year-olds in Head Start, smaller classes, buildings to house those classes, intensive tutoring, teacher development and increased teacher salaries. We would no longer be misled with charter schools and unconstitutional vouchers. (p. 14)

Promote high-efficacy teaching. Teachers who believe that they can have a positive impact on students are called *high-efficacy* teachers. High-efficacy teachers "increase student achievement by accepting students and their ideas, using praise rather than criticism, persevering with low achievers, and using their time effectively," whereas teachers who are low-efficacy "are less student-centered, spend less time on learning activities, 'give up' on low achievers, and use criticism more than high-efficacy teachers" (Eggen & Kauchak, 1999, p. 452). High-efficacy teacher behavior sets the stage for other, related, essential teaching skills including use of time, organization, and questioning, and result in greater learning and a sense of order in the classroom. Given the increasing awareness of the connection between the quality of the interaction between teachers and students, and student aggression and violence, the importance of high-efficacy teacher behavior takes on great importance. As may be expected, students who behave aggressively are more likely to be reprimanded by teachers. But when teachers' reprimands occur, they often serve to promote additional negative and noncompliant behavior by students who are at high risk for aggression. What may be an effective teacher intervention for students at lower risk for aggression (such as a teacher's reprimand) may spur aggressive behavior on the part of higher-risk students. Researchers Van Acker, Grant, and Henry (1996) of the University of Illinois at Chicago found that the interaction between teachers and students was in itself a critical risk factor, because teachers responded differently to different types of students. A teacher who is encouraging, supportive, and attentive to one student, for example, may be harsh or direct strong criticism toward another. The researchers found that harsh criticism and unpredictability serve to accelerate antisocial behavior within already-aggressive students. On the other hand, teachers who respond in a high-efficacy manner to all students do much in the way of instilling and reinforcing prosocial behavior and do not exacerbate potentially explosive situations.

Provide administrative support. Re-empowering teachers does not mean stepping up the already adversarial relationship sometimes seen between teachers and principals and always seen between unions and school boards. We all too frequently hear blame heaped on teachers' unions (or school boards) for being greedy, intransigent, and unconcerned with student welfare. Instead of taking sides in the fray, we must recognize that teachers' unions and school boards operate within an adversarial system— they are supposed to be adversaries in a system that works as a you-give-this-I'll-give-that but not as a collaborative endeavor. School boards and teachers' unions relate not in a mutual, community-oriented meeting of minds, but in a carefully arranged ritual of formalized conflict. As public employees, educators are already more vulnerable than doctors or lawyers to political and media pressure and thus must find a way to move out of that box and do their important work less encumbered and more empowered. One possible solution is to remove administrators from the adversarial paradigm—removing principals from, for example, negotiations between teachers' unions and school districts. That would more surely buttress the principals' credibility as an educational leader, increasing their value to the staff, school, and community. It is far better for students when their school district hires a lawyer to argue against teachers than to use the principal in that capacity. It is better, too, for teachers to hire a lawyer to fire back.

Restructure teacher preparation. There has been an increased concern about the quality of American teachers, arising in response to media-fanned fears that other nations' students achieve at higher levels than American students. Although many of the comparisons have been shown to be quite flawed, the misperception persists. Nevertheless, teachers, for better or worse, have a key role to play in making an impact on the serious social problems posed by antisocial behavior and violence. It makes good sense, then, to reorient teacher preparation programs to create a prosocial educational narrative. First, teacher education programs must include clear instruction for future teachers on classroom management as well as effective instructional strategies that will build student success. This will help empower teachers-as-experts in classroom leadership. Second, we must reach agreement on a few key high-efficacy teacher behaviors, teach those behaviors, and then identify teachers who demonstrate those behaviors. Third, student teachers should be assigned to work with these identified high-efficacy master teachers, learning, among other skills, how to *own* spaces and times in school. Once hired, new teachers should have a 2-year probationary period to demonstrate their ability to provide educational leadership in the classroom.

Best Community-Level Preventive Responses to Antisocial Behavior

Redevelop a Constructive, Prosocial, and Procommunity Narrative

Schools do not exist in a vacuum; each public school in America is part of a community. When there are serious problems in a community, those problems also find their way into the local schools. Measures to reduce antisocial behavior and violence can and must start at the school level, but the larger community must provide support for those measures. Ahead, I will discuss several key measures for reducing antisocial and violent behavior; each must be developed and fostered within the schools and community.

As mentioned earlier, schools are the best places each society has to address the need for socialization on the widest of scales. Alfie Kohn (1993) said that "prosocial values are learned in a community, and part of what is learned is the value of community" (p. 246). Kohn's truism notwithstanding, today's communities have perhaps never been in as disheveled a state as they are today. With mobility characterizing so many American (and world) communities, opponents of high-stakes standardized testing point out that in our urban areas, our annual comparisons of a school's test scores from year to year are invalid: Due to incredible turnover—students moving in and out of schools so frequently—test score comparisons are invalid because we are comparing completely different groups of students.

Coupled with the American embrace of legalism, which abhors community influence and social pressure, it is not surprising that the American public school is an ambivalent institution. It is missing a soul and mission, and this is related to the loss of soul and mission within our communities. There is an urgent need to restore to our communities and schools narratives of unity, identity, and cooperation as well as shared beliefs (narratives) that would give primacy to the constructive and unifying elements in diversity instead of the destructive effects of a legalistic, atomistic view of the individual's role in society. Daniel Callahan (1996), former president of The Hastings Center, described the problem of the law and morality: "Legalism may, then, be defined as the translation of moral problems into legal problems . . . and the elevation of the moral judgments of courts as the moral standards of the land." He concludes by describing how "there has come to be some enormous moral vacuum in this country, which for lack of better institutional candidates has been left to the law to fill." Callahan concludes that law ". . . may be the best institution we have, but it is a poor substitute for moral consensus and public debate on ethics." The time has certainly come for our schools to present themselves as "better institutional candidates"—the very places for us to come together for that moral consensus and public discussion to help fill the vacuum (p. 35).

To shore up the legitimacy of our schools' leaders, we must focus and use the force of the community (collective efficacy), harnessing the power of the neighborhood, and allow it to be, in turn, strengthened by its public school. Although we cannot turn back the clocks and eradicate huge, anonymous, suburban tracts and urban apartment buildings, we can locate and rejuvenate each community starting from its center, which is each public school in America. Churches and synagogues and other houses of worship presently provide this center on a smaller scale but mostly for their members or adherents. The public school can serve all members of a community. And the initiative to make schools the center of a community need not only involve neighborhood children and their parents. Allow me to relate a brief example of this initiative. Several years ago, when I was an elementary school principal, my school staff cooked up a plan to invite students' grandparents into school for the day, to share recess, to share lunch, and to share many of the joys that schools can provide. When we discovered that many of our students either had no living grandparent or had grandparents residing too far from the school to attend, we came up with an Adopt-a-Grandparent program. Our students without grandparents invited older men and women in the community to be their honorary grandparent for the day. It was enormously gratifying to see the lunch tables filled with young and old, senior citizens and junior citizens laughing and telling stories to each other. Remarkable things were noticed: Mark threw no food at anyone during lunch; Jason bullied no one during recess; Amber teased no one unmercifully. At the end of the day, many seniors thanked our teachers personally, saying that they had never before been invited to school, and others were surprised to see how little (or how much) schools had changed over the years. Still others were pleasantly surprised to see how their tax dollars were being spent, and a few managed to keep up an ongoing correspondence with their young, adopted, honorary grandchild. This is but one example of how schools can be put to better use to empower young and old and to build a procommunity, educational narrative. It is perhaps redundant to add that at the end of each of our ensuing (what became known as) Honorary Grandparent Days, teachers commented on how well behaved the children were. Remarked my amazed sixth-grade teacher, "Mark even held the door open for his guest!" Given what we know about connection, caring, and collective efficacy, it is not at all surprising that we witnessed this flip side of antisocial behavior, with its most powerful prosocial effects on Mark, Jason, and Amber.

Bring Education Funds Back to Schools From Prisons

There has been a virtual explosion of new prison construction to accommodate the almost 2 million Americans now incarcerated or awaiting trial. According to the Justice Policy Institute, this increase in spending for prisons has come at the expense of education. Writers for the Institute point out that most offenders are nonviolent; and 84% of the increase in state and federal prison rolls since 1980 comprises nonviolent offenders (Ambrosio & Schiraldi, 1997). In the 1980s, state spending on prisons increased 95% while education spending decreased 6%. This prison capacity has been excessive due to a build-'em and fill-'em policy. Today, California is spending more for its prisons than for its entire, extensive system of higher education. It is estimated that it costs $54,000 to build one new prison cell, and the cost of maintaining one California prisoner for 1 year is equal to the cost of educating five California state university students. Ambrosio and Schiraldi recommend an immediate, nationwide moratorium on the construction of new prisons. They argue that, at present, there is already far more than sufficient capacity to house every violent offender in America. They recommend that funds earmarked for new prison construction be diverted to create community correction programs that would allow $160 billion state general-fund dollars to go to education instead of toward increasing state and federal prison capacity.

Increase Media Moderation

Writing for the Justice Policy Institute, Kim Brooks, Vincent Schiraldi, and Jason Ziedenberg (2000) claim that Americans are "not just misinformed" but "exponentially misinformed, by the hyperbole that too often follows school shootings" (p. 22). Certainly, most Americans come to know violence not through personal experience but from what they get from the media. Since the first highly publicized school shooting in the 1980s, Americans have become more fearful of both children and schools to a degree that is out of proportion to the actual risk. With the rate of homicides dropping, with the crime rate dropping, and with school violence decreasing, most Americans nevertheless believe that a shooting is likely in their neighborhood school. Hundreds—perhaps thousands—of alarmist articles and sensational special reports have appeared on the Internet, television, and in the print media since the 1999 Columbine tragedy. The titles of these reports are provocative and ominous: "Did the Law Cause Columbine?" "What the Columbine Report Didn't Tell You," "Post-Columbine Fears Fuel School Style Wars," "Columbine Will Happen Again," and "Columbine Could Happen Again."

To help remedy this situation, Americans must demand media moderation, having news presented in context and shorn of sensational and hyperbolic language. The Justice Policy Institute asks that when a shooting occurs in or near a school, newscasters add that such shootings are not only exceedingly rare but are also not on the increase and that statistics show that serious violence in school continues to decline. The Institute asks that phrases such as *another in a series of school shootings* and *an all-too-common phenomenon* be dropped from newscasts. When there is a shooting or multiple murder at, for example, a fast-food restaurant or a religious institution, we do not hear newscasters warning that "there is an upward spiral of death" at fast-food restaurants or that churches and synagogues should be avoided, because they are places of "ever-increasing violence." Furthermore, few fast-food restaurants, churches, or synagogues would seriously consider responding with the installation of metal detectors or the hiring of armed guards.

There are hopeful signs that concerns expressed over media sensationalism are being heard: Out of a concern for what it called *mayhem* that was being televised, television station KVUE in Austin, Texas, adopted a five-criteria policy that determined whether or not they would cover crime stories on their evening news. The criteria: "(1) Does action need to be taken? (2) Is there an immediate threat to safety? (3) Is there a threat to children? (4) Does the crime have significant community impact? (5) Does the story lend itself to a crime prevention effort?" (Holley, 1996, n.p.). Regrettably, such intelligent, unhysterical criteria do not yet appear to be the rule throughout the news and entertainment industry.

Decide Which Way for Inclusion

Inclusion denotes the placing of students with disabilities in the regular classroom. However, some students' behavior is so seriously disordered that public schools are forced to place some of these students in special classes. In Seattle, students with severe antisocial behavior [also called *antisocial behavior disorder* (ABD)] are now being placed outside the regular classroom in specially created classrooms. Controversy exists as to whether or not these students are correctly placed, given the federal and state mandates on one hand and fiscal pressures on the other. Across the United States, the number of students who have been diagnosed with an emotional disturbance or emotional-behavioral disturbance has grown faster than any other special-education category. Accordingly, the pressures to include these children in the regular classroom are great despite the fact that even many experienced teachers have little preparation, support, and resources to respond to these placements. In a relatively few but perhaps increasing number of cases, a child's behavior is dangerous, causing teachers to worry about the safety of the child and the safety of other students. In states such as Vermont in which there is limited funding for special education, inclusion becomes full inclusion, and almost every special education student is routinely placed in the regular classroom. Due mostly to the expense involved in out-of-classroom placements, few of those otherwise-appropriate placements are made. With the swelling of numbers of students diagnosed as having an emotional disturbance, along with other, attendant horror stories (including the explosion of paperwork surrounding each placement), this problem has "reached a critical mass," as one special educator called it. When I was a school principal, my special education teachers were swamped with paperwork, spending less than half their work time actually working with students. I was able to convince the school board to hire an assistant. From my conversations today with principals and special education teachers, the situation has worsened. A public, community dialogue is long overdue as to how our public schools must address this situation for the sake of the teachers but, mostly, for the sake of the children and parents involved.

Get Rid of Weapons

Statistics on deaths and injuries of American children from weapons is depressing and bleak. The United States has the highest rate of murder of children among industrialized countries, and the overall rate of homicide by firearms was 16 times higher than the other countries' average (Reuters, 1997). In the 20-year period from 1979 to 1999, the number of U.S. children who have died from gunfire (60,008) exceeds the number of U.S. soldiers who lost their lives in the Gulf and Vietnam wars as well as in U.S. engagements in Haiti, Somalia, and Bosnia combined (Children's Defense Fund, 1997).

We need effective elimination of handguns instead of political gestures that are designed to alarm or to mollify the public or to deflect attention from the issue. Americans witness political harangues by and against the National Rifle Association, increased regulation and taxation of hunters, legislation mandating gun locks and background checks, and even litigation directed at handgun manufacturers to pay damages for deaths resulting from handguns they manufactured. These measures make it appear that something is being done about the problem, but all that seems to be accomplished is the enrichment of those who profit from advocating and pursuing litigation. Children have certainly not gained from these measures. Perhaps former New York state senator Daniel Moynihan (1993/1994) had a promising idea: Realizing that there was already a sufficient supply of guns to last for 200 years but only a 4-year supply of ammunition, the senator called for a law restricting the production of ammunition, saying, "Guns don't kill people . . . bullets do" (p. 18). In addition, America's communities need to take measures to reduce the number of handguns in the home and on the streets, handguns that are accessible and available to children, adolescents, and young adults.

Hill Walker (1998), codirector of the Institute on Violence and Destructive Behavior at the University of Oregon, offered the following thoughts on the challenge of violence:

> We have a violent history as a country and many experts argue that we are, by nature, a violent culture. As a society, we need to hold up a mirror and examine ourselves in this regard to take a good look at what we have become, how we got here and how we might change for the better . . . As we embark on a new century, we have the occasion to make a fresh start in this regard. (p. 1)

Summary

In conclusion, several broad issues must be addressed to best use our schools to meet the challenge of antisocial behavior. First, we must focus more attention on the connection between what is learned in school, and how it plays out outside of school. In other words, although schools are the safest of places for children and adolescents throughout the world, we do not yet have public awareness that the prosocial behavior students learn in school does, in fact, transfer outside of school. Along these lines, we must address the media-fanned erosion of public confidence in our schools' ability to make a positive contribution to our society and its individuals.

Larger social problems must be addressed, as these form the backdrop to much antisocial behavior and violence. In addition to addressing serious problems, such as the proliferation of guns, the increasing levels of poverty among children of America and the world, and the increasing alienation felt by millions of young students and nonstudents alike, we need to find a way for a public forum for such dialogues to take place. At present, educational and community decisions are made with little public input and even less public discussion. They are made by judges and courts and at the behest of special interest groups, by well-funded corporate interests. In 1960, before he left office, President Dwight Eisenhower warned Americans of the proliferation of the military-industrial complex. Today's problem is perhaps an even more serious one, as it involves the exclusion of the public from the democratic process through legal means. Through today's government-corporate complex, important decisions that affect the lives of Americans are made with no public input. To help turn this around, schools can provide the ideal locations to act locally, to have neighborhood-level discussions and dialogues take place. School buildings are already quite evenly distributed throughout the United States with respect to population, they are generally open to public use, and most are already accessible, familiar, community places. Government officials and elected officials could not easily ignore the dialogues of these neighborhood groups. Let us turn our public schools into places of parent, child, family, and neighbor inclusion and conversation rather than exclusion and incarceration.

As a first issue for dialogue, communities and schools might begin their discussion on what to do with children with severe behavior disorders. Although these youngsters appear to be placed more or less successfully in small classes such as those in Washington State, these are the exceptions rather than the rule. At present, the national and statewide dialogue (which is less of a dialogue and more of a top-down monologue) is obsessed with the wrong questions, questions about legalities and loopholes, such as "For how long can we suspend a child?" "How much should parents be fined when their children are truant?" (or, as in Michigan, Georgia, and other states, "For how long should parents be imprisoned when their children are truant?"), "Who can be sued when a gun is brought to school?" and "How young a child can be placed on trial as an adult?"

These questions may be of interest to the legal community and the news media, but in terms of socialization, they are trivial, irrelevant, and unconstructive responses to serious social issues. They may even be unethical questions, because they are directed in the wrong direction by the wrong people and at the wrong targets. For example, the students around whom these questions are posed tend overwhelmingly to be male, black, and poor, and to have typically grown up in abusive homes (Teichroeb, 1997). This group of students also has a high dropout rate (over 50%), and they are usually unemployed, with as many as 40% eventually acquiring a criminal record after dropping out. In the absence of an ethical discussion of what is truly in the best interests of these students and their role in society, the legal juggernaut continues to roll on, funneling these mostly male, black, and poor children out of schools and into an ever-expanding prison system. Aldous Huxley and George Orwell, authors of futuristic works of fiction, *Brave New World* and *1984,* respectively, would probably have dismissed this 21st-century, prison-filling scenario as too preposterous for readers to entertain. It is critical that we regain a perspective: We must not accept, and take for granted, that today's schools must serve as funnels to courts and prisons. Instead, schools should serve as means to *prevent* incarceration. This is done by recalling the original vision for our public schools: to educate our young so they can be productive adults and enjoy the fruits of full participation in a democratic society.

I am not advocating anarchy, only a stepping back from our embrace of legalism, which is growing increasingly distorted, roping off regions in which public input is impossible. (As I type this, I hear that lawyers in Florida and Texas are reaping $5 billion from tobacco lawsuits, and one Maryland lawyer is garnering $1.1 billion of Maryland's $4 billion tobacco settlement. These billions would buy a lot of medical care for expectant mothers and children, and medications and medical care for our elderly people, among a host of educational endeavors including the hiring of real teachers with college degrees for America's poorest students and families.)

We have been prevented from looking at and talking to one another and seeing the social solutions that are possible, solutions that include effective educational measures rather than legal or medical reactions to antisocial behavior. Certainly, some cases of violence are unexplainable and unpredictable and can only be dealt with through legal and medical measures. Nevertheless, many—perhaps most—acts of violence and antisocial behavior are preventable. Because we know how to prevent these acts, we have a moral obligation as well as a social obligation to move in that direction.

In effect, I believe the issue of what we as a society or nation or world can do toward educating our young people toward prosocial relations provides a more worthwhile challenge than figuring out how Americans can rank first in the world in science test scores, and more productive than debating which steroids should be legal for high school athletes to use and whether we should have one or 10 computers per student in school. Educator Robert Smilovitz (1996) warns that schools must place their social mission above all academic roles. He implores us to teach ourselves and our students, above all else, to attach the highest priority not to academia and technique but to our social relations with each other. He shares advice for educators provided by an anonymous friend who survived a concentration camp:

> Help your students to be human. Your efforts must never produce learned monsters, skilled psychopaths, or educated Eichmanns. Reading and writing and spelling and history and arithmetic are only important if they serve to make our students human. (p. 18)

References

Abate, F. R. (Ed.). (1999). *Oxford American Dictionary.* New York: Oxford University Press.

AIDS is leaving a generation of orphans. (2000, July 15). *The Labour Spokesman* (p. 15). Basseterre: Federation of St. Kitts & Nevis: St. Kitts-Nevis Labour Party.

Allais, C., & McKay, V. (1995). *A sociology of educating.* Johannesburg, SA: Lexicon.

Ambrosio, T., & Schiraldi, V. (1997). *From classrooms to cellblocks: A national perspective.* Washington, DC: The Justice Policy Institute. Retrieved August 15, 2000, from the Center on Juvenile and Criminal Justice from the World Wide Web: www.cjcj/org/jpi/highernational. html

Arnold, E. (1982). The use of corporal punishment in child rearing in the West Indies. *Child Abuse and Neglect: The International Journal, 6*(2), 141-145.

Astor, R., Meyer, H., & Behre, W. (1999). Unowned places and times: Maps and interviews about violence in high schools. *American Educational Research Journal, 36*(1), 3-42.

Atmore, E. (1993). *Providing early childhood EDUCARE services for the black pre-school child.* In J. LeRoux (Ed.), *The black child in crisis: A socio-educational perspective.* Pretoria, SA: Van Schaik.

Atmore, E. (1994). *Community and parent involvement in early childhood development: The South African experience.* Washington, DC: Clearinghouse No. PS022989. (ERIC Document Reproduction Service No. ED 380 195)

Azrin, H., Hake, D., Holz, W., & Hutchinson, R. (1965). Motivational aspects of escape from punishment. *Journal of the Experimental Analysis of Behavior, 8,* 31-34.

Badenhorst, D. C. (1998). The socializing role of the school. In E. Prinsloo & S. Du Plessis (Eds.), *Socio-Education II* (pp. 56-115). Pretoria: University of South Africa.

Balikci, A. (1970). *The Netsilik Eskimo.* Garden City, NY: Natural History Press.

Banks, R. (1997, April). Bullying in schools. *ERIC Digest.* Champaign, IL: ERIC Clearinghouse on Elementary and Early Childhood Education (ERIC Document Reproduction Service No. ED 407 154, 1-4). Retrieved May 30, 2000, from the ERIC Digest database from the World Wide Web: www.ed.gov/databases/ERIC_Digests/ed407154.html

Berard, R. M., Pringle, E. F., & Ahmed, N. (1997, Summer). A preliminary investigation of high-school counseling resources on the Cape Peninsula. *Adolescence, 32,* 373-379.

Berenson, A. (2000, April 16). Looking for a few honest lawyers. *New York Times,* p. 16WK.

Berkowitz, L. (1983). Aversively stimulated aggression: Some parallels and difference in research with animals and humans. *American Psychologist, 38,* 1135-1144.

Bernat, V. (1993). Teaching peace. *Young Children, 48*(3), 36-39.

Biglan, A. (1995). Translating what we know about the context of antisocial behavior into a lower prevalence of such behavior. *Journal of Applied Behavior Analysis, 28*(4), 479-492.

Bollag, B. (1999/2000). Romani children go to school. *American Educator, 23*(4), 30-37.

Botha, M. (1995). *Preference for television violence and aggression among children from various South African townships: A follow-up study over two years.* Pretoria, SA: Human Sciences Research Council.

Botha, T. R. (1977). *Die sosiale lewe van die kind in opvoeding* [Teaching to the social life of the child] (pp. 121-126). Pretoria, SA: Pretoria Drukkers.

Bowlby, J. (1980). *Attachment and loss* (Vol. 3). New York: Basic Books.

Bracey, G. W. (1994). The fourth Bracey Report on the condition of public education. *Phi Delta Kappan, 79,* 114-127.

Brener, N. D., Simon, T. R., Krug, E. G., & Lowry, R. (1999). Recent trends in violence-related behaviors among high school students in the United States. *Journal of the American Medical Association, 282*(5), 440-446.

Brooks, K., Schiraldi, V., & Ziedenberg, J. (2000). *School house hype: Two years later.* Justice Policy Institute/Children's Law Center of the Center on Juvenile and Criminal Justice. Retrieved June 14, 2000, from the Center on Juvenile and Criminal Justice from the World Wide Web: www.cjcj.org/schoolhousehype/shh2.html

Buka, S., & Earls, F. (1993). Early determinants of delinquency and violence. *Health Affairs, 12*(2), 46-64.

Burnett, C. (1998). School violence in an impoverished South African community. *Child Abuse & Neglect: The International Journal, 22*(8), 789-796.

Butterfield, F. (1997, August 17). Study links violence rate to cohesion in community. *New York Times,* p. 27.

Callahan, D. (1996, November/December). Escaping from legalism: Is it possible? *Hastings Center Report, 26,* 34-35.

Carlsson-Paige, N., & Levin, D. (1985). *Helping young children understand peace, war and the nuclear threat.* Washington, DC: Association for Supervision and Curriculum Development.

Center, D. B., Deitz, S. M., & Kaufman, M. E. (1982). Student ability, task difficulty, and inappropriate classroom behavior: A study of children with behavior disorders. *Behavior Modification, 6,* 355-374.

Centers for Disease Control and Prevention. (1994). Health risk behaviors among adolescents who do and do not attend school: United States, 1992. *Morbidity Mortality Weekly Report, 43*(8), 129-132.

Centers for Disease Control and Prevention. (1999). *Facts about violence among youth and violence in schools.* CDC Media Relations. Atlanta, GA: Author. Retrieved August 5, 2000, from the Centers for Disease Control from the World Wide Web: www.cdc.gov/od/oc/media/fact/violence.htm

Charach, A., Pepler, D., & Zeigler, S. (1995). Bullying at school—a Canadian perspective: A survey of problems and suggestions for intervention. *Education Canada, 35*(1), 12-18.

Children's Defense Fund. (1997, March 23). *Gun deaths.* Retrieved January 31, 2000, from the World Wide Web: www.childrensdefense.org/safefaqs.html

Chomsky, N. (1994). *The prosperous few and the restless many.* Berkeley, CA: Odonian.

Cockburn, A. (1996, June 3). The war on kids. *The Nation,* 7-8.

Commercial Travelers Mutual Insurance Company. (2000-2001). *Student insurance plans 2000-2001: Why you need student insurance. . . .* [Brochure]. Utica, NY: Author.

Constas, M. A. (1997, Summer). Apartheid and the socio-political context of education in South Africa: A narrative account. *Teachers College Record, 98,* 682-720.

Craig, G. J. (1983). *Human development.* Englewood Cliffs, NJ: Prentice Hall.

Curwin, R. I. (1995, February). A humane approach to reducing violence in schools. *Educational Leadership,* 72-75.

Darling-Hammond, L. (1995). Restructuring schools for student success. *Daedalus: Journal of the American Academy of Arts and Sciences, 124*(4), 153-162.

deBary, W. T., Chan, W., & Tan, C. (1960). *Sources of Chinese tradition* (Vol. 1). New York: Columbia University Press.

DeMitchell, T. A., & Fossey, R. (1997). *Vain hopes and false promises: The limits of law-based school reform.* Lancaster, PA: Technomic.

DiGiulio, R. C. (1999). Non-violent interventions in secondary schools: Administrative perspectives. In L. R. Forcey & I. M. Harris (Eds.),

Peacebuilding for adolescents: Strategies for educators and community leaders (pp. 195-212). New York: Peter Lang.

DiGiulio, R. C. (2000). *Positive classroom management: A step-by-step guide to successfully running the show without destroying student dignity.* Thousand Oaks, CA: Corwin.

Dill, V. S., & Haberman, M. (1995, February). Building a gentler school. *Educational Leadership, 52*(5), 69-71.

Dodd, A. W. (2000). Making schools safe for all students: Why schools need to teach more than the 3 R's. *NASSP Bulletin, 84*(614), 25-31.

Doland, A. (2000). Violence shuts French schools. *Yahoo! News.* Retrieved January 25, 2000, from the Internet: dailynews.yahoo.com/h/ap/200000125/wl/france_school_violence_1.html

Dorfman, L, Woodruff, K., Chavez, V., & Wallack, L. (1997, August). Youth and violence on local television news in California. *American Journal of Public Health, 87*(8), 1311-1316.

Doyle, W. (1986). Classroom organization and management. In M. Wittrock (Ed.), *Handbook of research on teaching* (3rd ed., pp. 392-431). New York: Macmillan.

Dunkin, M. J., & Barnes, J. (1986). Research on teaching in higher education. In M. Wittrock (Ed.), *Handbook of research on teaching* (3rd ed., pp. 754-777). New York: Macmillan.

Durkheim, É. (1951). *Suicide.* New York: Free Press. (Original work published 1898)

Durkheim, É. (1961). *Moral education* (E. K. Wilson & H. Schnurer, Trans.). New York: Free Press. (Original work published 1925)

Eggen, P., & Kauchak, D. (1999). *Educational psychology* (4th ed.). Upper Saddle River, NJ: Simon & Schuster.

Eisenberg, N., & Mussen, P. (1989). *The roots of prosocial behavior in children.* Cambridge, UK: Cambridge University Press.

Elias, M. (2000, March 8). Bossier preschool kids are healthier. *USA Today,* p. D6.

Fanning, A. (2000, March 7). Parents have an obligation to be good sports, too. *USA Today,* p. C10.

Feldman, S. S., & Weinberger, D. A. (1994). Self-restraint as a mediator of family influences on boys' delinquent behavior: A longitudinal study. *Child Development, 65,* 195-211.

Fitzclarence, L. (1995). Education's shadow? Towards an understanding of violence in schools. *Australian Journal of Education, 39*(1), 22-40.

Fitzsimmons, M. K. (1998). Violence and aggression in children and youth. *ERIC/OSEP Digest E572.* Reston, VA: ERIC Clearinghouse on Disabilities and Gifted Education (ERIC Document Reproduction Service No. ED 429 19-98, 1-4). Retrieved June 23, 1999, from the ERIC Digest database from the World Wide Web: www.ed.gov/databases/ERIC_Digests/ed429419.html

Flexner, S. B. (Ed.). (1987). *The Random House dictionary of the English language* (2nd ed.). New York: Random House.

Foster, G. (1999, October 6). Brutality in the name of God. *Teacher/Daily Mail & Guardian,* Johannesburg, SA. Retrieved November 18, 1999, from the World Wide Web: www.teacher.co.za

Fuligni, A., & Eccles, J. (1993). Perceived parent-child relationships and early adolescents' orientation toward peers. *Developmental Psychology (15),* 622-632.

Fung, Y. (1966). *A short history of Chinese philosophy.* (E. Bodde, Ed.). New York: Free Press/McMillan.

Galper, J. (1998, March 1). Schooling for society: A swiftly changing scene. *American Demographics.* Retrieved March 30, 2000, from the Internet: britannica.com/bcom/magazine/article/0,5744,34599,00.html

Garson, P. (2000, January 6). Vision for a new era. *Teacher/Daily Mail & Guardian,* Johannesburg, SA. Retrieved January 13, 2000, from the World Wide Web: www.teacher.co.za

Gladden, R. M. (1998). The small schools movement: A review of the literature. In M. Fine & J. I. Somerville (Eds.), *Small schools, big imaginations* (p. 116). Chicago: Cross City Campaign for Urban School Reform.

Glassner, B. (1999, August 13). School violence: The fears, the facts. *New York Times on the Web.* Retrieved August 20, 1999, from the World Wide Web: www.nytimes.com/yr/mo/day/oped/13glas.html

Goodlad, J. I. (1984). *A place called school.* New York: McGraw-Hill.

Goodman, D. (1999). *Fault lines: Journeys into the new South Africa.* Berkeley: University of California Press.

Gorer, G. (1965). The pornography of death. In G. Gorer (Ed.), *Death, grief and mourning* (pp. 192-199). Garden City, NY: Doubleday.

Gormly, A. V. (1997). *Lifespan human development* (6th ed.). London: Harcourt Brace.

Greene, M. W. (1999). Redefining school violence in Boulder Valley, Colorado. In L. R. Forcey & I. M. Harris (Eds.), *Peacebuilding for adolescents: Strategies for educators and community leaders* (pp. 57-88). New York: Peter Lang.

Grey, J. (2000, January 6). No food, no shoes, no school. *Teacher/Daily Mail & Guardian,* Johannesburg, SA. Retrieved July 25, 2000, from the World Wide Web: www.teacher.co.za/200001/poverty.html

Grossman, D., Neckerman, H., Koepsall, T., Liu, P. Y., Asher, K. N., Beland, K., Frey, K., & Rivara, F. P. (1997). The effectiveness of a violence prevention curriculum among children in elementary school: A randomized controlled trial. *Journal of the American Medical Association, 277*(20), 1605-1611.

Gumbi, B. E. (1995). The black high school principal's role in a political transition in South Africa. *Dissertation Abstracts International, 56*(03A), 0777.

Gurian, M. (2000). Helping boys become men. *National Retired Teachers Association Bulletin, 41*(3), 18-21.

Haberman, M. (1997). Unemployment training: The ideology of nonwork learned in urban schools. *Phi Delta Kappan, 78*(7), 499-503.

Hamber, B. (1998). Dr Jekyll and Mr. Hyde: problems of violence prevention and reconciliation in South Africa's transition to democracy. In E. Bornman, R. van Eeden, & M. Wentzel (Eds.), *Perspectives on aggression and violence in South Africa*. Pretoria, SA: Human Sciences Research Council.

Hammond, S. (2000, March 16). Looking for alternatives to corporal punishment. *Teacher/Daily Mail & Guardian,* Johannesburg, SA. Retrieved March 23, 2000, from the World Wide Web: www.teacher.co.za/ 200003/ corporal.html

Harris, I. M. (1999). A summer institute on nonviolence. In L. R. Forcey & I. M. Harris (Eds.), *Peacebuilding for adolescents: Strategies for educators and community leaders* (pp. 309-329). New York: Peter Lang.

Harris, I. M. (2000). Peace-building responses to school violence. *NASSP Bulletin, 84*(614), 5-24.

Hartley, W. S. (1977). Preventive outcomes of affective education with school age children: An epidemiologic follow-up of the Kansas City School Behavior Project. In D. C. Klein & S. E. Goldston (Eds.), *Primary prevention: An idea whose time has come* (pp. 69-75). Washington, DC: Government Printing Office.

Hawkins, J. D., Farrington, D. P., & Catalano, R. F. (1998). Reducing violence through the schools. In D. Elliott, B. Hamburg, & K. Williams (Eds.), *Violence in American schools: A new perspective*. Cambridge, UK: Cambridge University Press.

Holley, J. (1996, May/June). Should the coverage fit the crime? *Columbia Journalism Review*. Retrieved February 22, 1999, from the World Wide Web: www.cjr.org/year/96/3/coverage.asp

Howard, E. R. (1981). School climate improvement: Rationale and process. *Illinois School Research and Development, 18*(1), 8-12.

Human Services Research Council. (1981). *Report of the Work Committee: Guidance*. Pretoria, SA: Author.

Hutchinson, R. (1977). By-products of aversive control. In W. K. Honig & J.E.R. Staddon (Eds.), *Handbook of operant behavior* (pp. 415-431). Englewood Cliffs, NJ: Prentice Hall.

Hyman, I., & Perone, D. (1998). The other side of school violence: Educator policies and practices that may contribute to student misbehavior. *Journal of School Psychology, 36*(1), 7-27.

Internet Movie Database. (2000). Plot outline for *Teacher's Pet (1930)*. Retrieved August 27, 2000, from the Internet: us.imdb.com/Title?0021456

Internet Movie Database. (2000). Plot outline for *Teacher's Pet (2000/I)*. Retrieved August 27, 2000, from the Internet: us.imdb.com/Title?0217086

Johnson, K. (2000, February 28). Youths in adult prisons double. *USA Today,* p. A1.

Jones, C. (1999, August 4). Back to school, guardedly. *USA Today,* pp. A1, A2.

Josephson Institute on Ethics. (1999). *1998 report card on the ethics of American youth: Survey data on youth violence.* Retrieved May 30, 2000, from the World Wide Web: www.josephsoninstitute.org/98-Survey/violence/98survey-violence.htm

Kauffman, J., & Burbach, H. (1997). On creating a climate of classroom civility. *Phi Delta Kappan, 79*(4), 320-325.

Kelleher, K. J., McInerny, T. K., Gardner, W. P., Childs, G. E., & Wasserman, R. C. (2000, June). Increasing identification of psychosocial problems: 1979-1996. *Pediatrics, 105*(6), 1313-1321.

Kennel-Shank, C. (2000). School house lock. *Sojourners, 29*(1), 49.

Keogh, B. K. (1998). Classrooms as well as students deserve study. *Remedial and Special Education, 19*(6), 313-314.

Key California votes. (2000, March 8). *USA Today,* p. A12.

Kidder, R. M. (2000, April 3). Ethics is not a luxury; it's essential to our survival. *Education Week on the Web.* Retrieved April 7, 2000, from the World Wide Web: www.edweek.org/ew/vol-10/10210010.h10

Kielburger, C. (1998). *Free the children.* New York: HarperCollins.

King, C. I. (2000, March 11). What every child needs [Letter to the editor]. *New York Times,* p. A19.

Klein, D. C., & Goldston, S. E. (1977). Preface. In D. C. Klein & S. E. Goldston (Eds.), *Primary prevention: An idea whose time has come* (p. vii). Washington, DC: Government Printing Office.

Kohn, A. (1993). *Punished by rewards.* Boston: Houghton Mifflin.

Kurdek, L., & Fine, M. (1994). Family acceptance and family control as predictors of adjustment in young adolescents: Linear, curvilinear, or interactive effects. *Child Development 65,* 1137-1146.

Lamborn, S., Mounts, N., Steinberg, L., & Dornbusch, S. (1991). Patterns of competence and adjustment among adolescents from authoritative, authoritarian, indulgent, and neglectful families. *Child Development, 62,* 1049-1065.

Landman, W. (1992). A perception of national party policy regarding education. In C. Heese & D. Badenhorst (Eds.), *South Africa: The education equation* (pp. 23-27). Pretoria, SA: J. L. van Schaik.

Langdon, C. A., & Vesper, N. (2000). The sixth Phi Delta Kappa poll of teachers' attitudes toward the public schools. *Phi Delta Kappan, 81,* 607-611.

Lantieri, L. (1995). Waging peace in our schools: Beginning with the children. *Phi Delta Kappan, 76*(5), 386-388.

Lenihan, P. (2000, February 2). Boys' aggressive behavior rewarded with popularity. *Education Week on the Web.* Retrieved February 10, 2000, from the World Wide Web: www.edweek.org/ew/ewstory.cfm?slug=21report.h19

Lipscomb, T., MacAllister, H., & Bregman, N. (1985). A developmental inquiry into the effects of multiple models on children's generosity. *Merrill-Palmer Quarterly, 31,* 585-589.

Lockwood, D. (1997). Violence among middle school and high school students: Analysis and implications for prevention. *National Institute of Justice Research in Brief* (Publication NCJ 166363, pp. 1-9). Washington, DC: U.S. Department of Justice.

MacDonald, I., & da Costa, J. (1996, June). *Exploring issues of school violence: "The code of silence."* Paper presented at the annual meeting of the Canadian Association for the Study of Educational Administration, St. Catharines, Ontario, Canada.

Magau, T. (1999). Teachers' perceptions about their participation in decision-making: An international comparison of two schools (South Africa, United States). *Dissertation Abstracts International, 60*(01A), 0036.

Main, M., & George, C. (1985). Responses of abused and disadvantaged toddlers to distress in agemates: A study in the day-care setting. *Developmental Psychologist, 21,* 407-413.

Mamabolo, C. S. (1997). Teacher education and the professional status of the teacher in the Northern Province (South Africa). *Masters Abstracts International, 36*(3), 0670.

Manlove, D. C., & Elliott, P. (1979). Absent teachers: Another handicap for students? *The Practitioner, 5,* 2-3.

Marjoribanks, K., & Mboya, M. M. (1998). Factors affecting the self-concepts of South African students. *Journal of Social Psychology, 138*(5), 572-580.

Martin, J. R. (1992). *The schoolhome.* Cambridge, MA: Harvard University Press.

Maslow, A. (1970). *Motivation and personality.* New York: Harper & Row.

Massey, M. S. (1998). Early childhood violence prevention. *ERIC Digest.* Champaign, IL: Clearinghouse on Elementary and Early Childhood Education. (ERIC Document Reproduction Service No. ED 424 032)

Mayer, G. R. (1995). Preventing antisocial behavior in the schools. *Journal of Applied Behavior Analysis, 28,* 467-478.

Mayer, G. R., Butterworth, T., Komoto, T., & Benoit, R. (1983). The influence of the school principal on the consultant's effectiveness. *Elementary School Guidance and Counseling, 17,* 274-279.

Mayer, G. R., & Sulzer-Azaroff, B. (1991). Interventions for vandalism. In G. Stoner, M. K. Shinn, & H. M. Walker (Eds.), *Interventions for achievement and behavior problems* (pp. 559-580). Washington, DC: National Association of School Psychologists.

Mboya, M. M. (1995). Variations in parenting practices: Gender- and age-related differences in African adolescents. *Adolescence, 30,* 955-962.

McLean, M. M. (1995). It's a Blackboard Jungle out there: The impact of media and film on the public's perceptions of violence in the schools. *English Journal, 84*(5), 19-21.

Menninger, K. (1968). *The crime of punishment.* New York: Viking.

Mercy, J. A., Rosenberg, M. L., Powell, K. E., Broome, C. V., & Roper, W. L. (1993). Public health policy for preventing violence. *Health Affairs, 12*(2), 7-29.

Metropolitan Life Insurance Company. (1993). *The Metropolitan Life survey of the American teacher 1993: Violence in America's public schools.* New York: Author.

Montessori, M. (1988). *The absorbent mind.* Oxford, UK: Clio Press.

Moynihan, D. P. (1993/1994). Defining deviancy down: How we've become accustomed to alarming levels of crime and destructive behavior. *American Educator, 17*(4), 10-18.

Munk, D. D., & Repp, A. C. (1994). The relationship between instructional variables and problem behavior: A review. *Exceptional Children, 60,* 390-401.

Murray, J. P. (1995). Children and television in violence. *Kansas Journal of Law and Public Policy, 4*(3), 7-14.

National Education Policy Investigation. (1992). *Support services.* Cape Town, SA: Oxford University Press.

National Institute of Mental Health. (1982). *Television and behavior: Ten years of scientific progress and implications for the eighties* (Vol. 1). (Department of Health & Human Services Publication No. ADM 82-1195). Washington, DC: Government Printing Office.

National Television Violence Study. (1996-1998). *National Television Violence Study* (Vols. 1-3). Thousand Oaks, CA: Sage.

Neal, D., & Kirp, D. L. (1986). The allure of legalization reconsidered: The case of special education. In D. L. Kirp & D. N. Jensen (Eds.), *School days, rule days: The legalization and regulation of education.* Philadelphia: Falmer.

New Florida laws effective July 1. (2000, June 30). *Daytona Beach [Florida] News-Journal.* Retrieved June 30, 2000, from the World Wide Web: www.news-journalOn-line.com/2000/Jun/30/FLA8.htm

Niebel, G. (1994). Violence and aggression in schools in Schleswig-Holstein. *Zeitschrift fur Padagogik, 39*(5), 775-798. Washington, DC: U.S. Department of Education. (ERIC Document Reproduction Service No. EJ 496 931)

Noddings, N. (1996). Learning to care and to be cared for. In A. M. Hoffman (Ed.), *Schools, violence, and society.* Westport, CT: Praeger.

Noguera, P. A. (1995). Preventing and producing violence: A critical analysis of responses to school violence. *Harvard Educational Review, 65*(2), 189-212.

Novicki, M. (1991, May-June). John Samuel: Ending apartheid. *African Report,* 18-22.

Ohsako, T. (Ed.). (1997). Violence at school: Global issues and interventions. Paris: UNESCO, International Bureau of Education.

Olweus, D. (1995, December). Bullying or peer abuse at school: Facts and intervention. *Current Directions, 4,* 196-200.

O'Neill, B. (1994, March 6). The history of a hoax. *New York Times Magazine,* pp. 46-49.

Ornstein, A. C., & Levine, D. U. (2000). *Foundations of education.* Boston: Houghton Mifflin.

Orr, D. (1994, June). Building a new South African society. *Choices (New York), 3,* 12-17.

Periscope: Newsweek.com Live vote. (2000, March 13). *Newsweek,* p. 6.

Phillips, M. F. (2000, May 14). Paying to fix schools [Letter to the editor]. *New York Times,* p. 14WK.

Plucker, J. A. (2000). Positive approaches to preventing school violence: Peace building in schools and communities. *NASSP Bulletin, 84*(614), 1-4.

Polk, K, & Schaefer, W. E. (Eds.). (1972). *Schools and delinquency.* Englewood Cliffs, NJ: Prentice Hall.

Postman, N. (1993). *Technopoly: The surrender of culture to technology.* New York: Vintage.

Prinsloo, E., & Du Plessis, S. (1998). *Socio-education I.* Pretoria: University of South Africa, Department of Educational Studies.

Prinsloo, E., Vorster, P. J., & Sibaya, P. T. (1996). *Teaching with confidence: Psychology of education for Southern Africa.* Pretoria, SA: Kagiso Tertiary.

Prinsloo, J. (1994, November). *Corporal punishment in schools and fundamental human rights: A South African perspective.* Paper presented at the 40th annual meeting of the National Organization on Legal Problems in Education, San Diego, California.

Prothrow-Stith, D., & Quaday, S. (1995). *Hidden causalities: The relationship between violence and learning.* Washington, DC: National Health & Education Consortium and National Consortium for African American Children, U.S. Department of Education. (ERIC Document Reproduction Service No. ED 390 552)

Pont-Brown, M., & Krumboltz, J. (1999). Countering school violence: The rise of conflict resolution programs. In L. R. Forcey & I. M. Harris (Eds.), *Peacebuilding for adolescents: Strategies for educators and community leaders.* (pp. 35-55). New York: Peter Lang.

Quaglia, R. J. (2000). Making an impact on student aspirations: A positive approach to school violence. *NASSP Bulletin, 84*(614), 56-60.

Rapoport, R., Rapoport, R. N., & Strelitz, Z. (1977). *Fathers, mothers and society: Perspectives on parenting.* New York: Vintage

Raywid, M. A., & Oshiyama, L. (2000). Musings in the wake of Columbine: What can schools do? *Phi Delta Kappan, 81*(6), 444-449.

Reissland, N. (1988). Neonatal imitation in the first hour of life: Observations in rural Nepal. *Developmental Psychology, 24,* 464-469.

Reuters World News. (1996, February 17). Singapore says delinquency up. *Boston Globe,* p. 4.

Reuters World News. (1997, February 7). U.S. has highest rate of child murders. *Yahoo! News.* Retrieved June 14, 2000, from the Internet: yahoo.com/headlines/970207/news/stories/children_1.html

Reuters World News. (1999, October 1). Nigeria launches free education program, *Yahoo! News.* Retrieved October 1, 1999, from the Internet: uk.news.yahoo.com/991001/1/8ntz.html

Reuters World News. (2000, February 23). Study says more U.S. kids given psychotropic drugs. *Yahoo! News.* Retrieved February 23, 2000, from the Internet: dailynews.yahoo.com/h/nm/20000223/ts/health_preschoolers_1.html

Robins, R., John, O., Caspi, A., Moffitt, T., & Stouthamer-Loeber, M. (1996). Resilient, overcontrolled, and undercontrolled boys: Three replicable personality types. *Journal of Personality and Social Psychology, 70,* 157-171.

Rodkin, P. C., Farmer, T. W., Pearl, R., & Van Acker, R. (2000). Heterogeneity of popular boys: Antisocial and prosocial configurations. *Developmental Psychology, 36*(1), 14-24.

Rohner, R. P. (1975). *They love me, they love me not: A world-wide study of the effects of parental acceptance and rejection.* New Haven, CT: Human Relations Area Files.

Rose, L. C., & Gallup, A. M. (1999). The 31st annual Phi Delta Kappa/Gallup poll of the public's attitudes toward the public schools. *Phi Delta Kappan, 81*(1), 41-56.

Sack, J. L. (1999, October 27). An ounce of prevention. *Education Week,* 32-33.

Sakurai, J. (1999). Violence among Japanese youth rises. *Yahoo! News.* Retrieved August 13, 1999, from the Internet: dailynews.yahoo.com/h/ap/19990813/wl/japan_youth_1.html

Sampson, R. J., Raudenbush, S. W., & Earls, F. (1997, August 15). Neighborhoods and violent crime: A multilevel study of collective efficacy. *Science,* 918-924.

Schuster, K. (1997, March 30). Schools suspend trio. *New Haven [Connecticut] Register,* p. 1.

Schwartz, W. (1999). Developing social competence in children. *Choices in preventing youth violence.* New York: Institute for Urban and Minority Education, Teachers College, Columbia University. Retrieved February 1, 2000, from the Internet: iume.tc.columbia.edu/choices/briefs/choices03.html

Shapiro, J. P. (1999). The Peacemakers Program: Effective violence prevention for early adolescent youth. *Communiqué.* Bethesda, MD: National Association of School Psychologists.

Siegel, L. J., & Senna, J. J. (1997). *Juvenile delinquency: Theory, practice, and law.* New York: West.

Skiba, R., & Peterson, R. (1999a). The dark side of zero tolerance: Can punishment lead to safe schools? *Phi Delta Kappan, 80,* 372-382.

Skiba, R., & Peterson, R. (1999b). Zap zero tolerance. *Education Digest,* 64(8), 24-30.

Smilovitz, R. (1996). *If not now, when? Education, not schooling.* Kearney, NE: Morris.

Smith, C. (1999, November 9). Breaking the culture of silence. *Teacher/Daily Mail & Guardian,* Johannesburg, SA. Retrieved November 9, 1999, from the World Wide Web: www.teacher.co.za

Snowman, J., Biehler, R., & Bonk, C. J. (2000). *Psychology applied to teaching.* Boston: Houghton Mifflin.

Snyder, H. N., & Sickmund, M. (1999). *Juvenile offenders and victims: 1999 national report.* Washington, DC: Office of Juvenile Justice and Delinquency Prevention.

South Africa Online. (1999). Mental Health Awareness Month/Possible action steps. Retrieved November 15, 2000, from the World Wide Web: www.southafrica.co/za/health/storie.html

South African Police Service. (2000, April). The monthly bulletin on reported crime in South Africa 4/2000. Retrieved November 15, 2000, from the World Wide Web: www.saps.co/za/8_crimeinfo/bulletin/2000(4).htm

Spuck, D. W. (1974). Reward structure in the public school. *Educational Administration Quarterly, 1,* 18-34.

Squelch, J. M. (1998). Children's rights. In E. Prinsloo & S. Du Plessis (Eds.), *Socio-Education II,* (pp. 116-130). Pretoria: University of South Africa.

Stein, L., & Mulrine, A. (1999). Do you know where your children are? *U.S. News and World Report, 126,* 17, 22-23.

Steinberg, L. (1999). *Adolescence* (5th ed.). Boston: McGraw-Hill.

Stevahn, L., Johnson, D., Johnson, R., & Real, D. (1996). The impact of a cooperative or individualistic contest on the effectiveness of conflict resolution training. *American Educational Research Journal, 33*(3), 801-823.

Storring, V. (Producer), & Zaritsky, J. (Director). (2000). Little criminals: Can a child be changed? *PBS Frontline.* Boston: WGBH. Retrieved May 15, 2000, from the Public Broadcasting Service from the World Wide Web: www.pbs.org/wgbh/pages/frontline/shows/little/readings/oregonlc.html

Straker, G. (1996). Violent political contexts and the emotional concerns of township youth. *Child Development, 67*(1), 46-64.

Stroman, C. A. (1991, Summer). Television's role in the socialization of African American children and adolescents. *Journal of Negro Education,* 314-326.

Suransky-Dekker, C. 1997. *Portraits of black schooling in South Africa.* Washington, DC: U.S. Department of Education. (ERIC Document Reproduction Service No. ED 412 619)

Tadesse, A. (1997, October). *Reforming juvenile justice legislation and administration in South Africa: A case study.* Paper presented at the International Seminar on Juvenile Justice at the UNICEF International Child Development Centre, Florence, Italy.

Takahashi, S., & Inoue, W. (1995). An essay on school violence and safety education in Japan. *Thresholds in Education, 21*(2), 26-28.

Talbot, N. (Ed.). (1976). *Raising children in modern America.* Boston: Little, Brown.

Taylor, R. (1998, July-August). Media 101. *Brill's Content*, 78-79.

Teichroeb, R. (1997, December 15). Problem students strain system. *Register Guard.* Retrieved January 4, 2000, from the Oregon Social Learning Center from the World Wide Web: www.oslc.org/InTheNews/probstuds.html

Thayer-Bacon, B. J. (1999). How can caring help? A personalized cross-generational examination of violent adolescent experiences in school. In L. R. Forcey & I. M. Harris (Eds.), *Peacebuilding for adolescents: Strategies for educators and community leaders* (pp. 139-160). New York: Peter Lang.

Tierno, M. (1996, Winter). Teaching as modeling: The impact of teacher behavior upon student character formation. *Educational Forum, 60,* 174-180.

Toby, J. (1993/1994, Winter). Everyday school violence: How disorder fuels it. *American Educator,* 4-9, 44-48.

United Nations Educational, Scientific, and Cultural Organization. (1994). *UNESCO statistical yearbook 1994* (pp. 2.26-2.27). Paris: Author.

U.S. Department of Education. (1998). *Violence and discipline problems in United States public schools: 1996-1997.* (NCES Publication No. NCES 98-030). Washington, DC: National Center for Educational Statistics.

U.S. Department of Justice, Federal Bureau of Investigation. (1993). *Crime in the United States: Uniform crime reports.* Washington, DC: Author.

U.S. Department of Justice: Federal Bureau of Investigation. (1996). *Crime in the United States: Uniform crime reports.* Washington, DC: Author.

U.S. Department of Justice, Federal Bureau of Investigation. (1998). *Crime in the United States: Uniform crime reports.* Washington, DC: Author.

U.S. Department of Justice, Office of Justice Programs. (1995). Evaluation of violence prevention programs in middle schools. *National Institute of Justice Update.* Washington, DC: Author.

U.S. Department of State. (1999a, May). *Fact sheet: Behavior modification facilities.* Consular information sheets and travel warnings. Retrieved June 1, 1999, from the Internet: travel.state.gov/behavior_modification.html

U.S. Department of State. (1999b, September 14). *South Africa consular information sheet.* Retrieved September 30, 1999, from the Internet: travel.state.gov/safrica.html

Van Acker, R., Grant, S. H., & Henry, D. (1996, August). Teacher and student behavior as a function of risk for aggression. *Education and Treatment of Children, 19,* 316-334.

van Eeden, R. (1996, August). *School violence: Psychologists' perspective.* Paper presented at the 104th annual meeting of the American Psychological Association, Toronto, Canada.

van't Westende, F. M. L. (1998). Juvenile delinquency. In E. Prinsloo & S. Du Plessis (Eds.), *Socio-Education II* (pp. 261-284). Pretoria: University of South Africa.

Vicini, J. (2000, May 7). Violent crime fell sharply again in 1999—FBI. *Reuters World News.* Retrieved May 10, 2000, from the Internet: dailynews.yahoo. com/htx/nm/200002507/ts/crime_fbi_1.html

Vuchinich, S., Bank, L., & Patterson, G. R. (1992). Parenting, peers, and stability of antisocial behavior in preadolescent boys. *Developmental Psychology, 28,* 518-521.

Wackenhut Corrections Corporation. (1999, July 27). *Wackenhut Corrections signs agreement for 3,024-bed prison in South Africa* [Company press release]. Palm Beach Gardens, FL: Author.

Walker, H. (1998, May 31). Youth violence: Society's problem. *[Eugene, Oregon] Register-Guard.* Retrieved April 28, 2000, from the Oregon Social Learning Center on the World Wide Web: www.oslc.org/InTheNews/society.html

Wallechinsky, D., & Wallace, I. (1975). *The people's almanac.* New York: Doubleday.

Webster, D. W. (1993). The unconvincing case for school-based conflict resolution programs for adolescents. *Health Affairs, 12*(4), 126-140.

Welsh, P. (1999). The price of protection: Protecting schools from violence. *U.S. News and World Report, 126,* 17-18.

Whitmire, R. (1994, January 11). Study finds early steps critical to halting violence. *Burlington [Vermont] Free Press,* p. 10A.

Wilkinson, D. Y. (1999). Integration dilemmas in a racist culture. In W. Noll (Ed.), *Taking sides: Clashing views on controversial education issues* (pp. 126-132). Guilford, CT: Dushkin/McGraw-Hill.

Witty, P. (1950). Children's, parents' and teachers' reactions to television. *Elementary English, 27*(6), 349-355, 396.

Wolfgang, C. H. (1995). *Solving discipline problems.* Boston: Allyn & Bacon.

Wong, E. (2000, August 13). Poorest schools lack teachers and computers. *New York Times,* p. NE14.

Youssef, R. W., Attia, M. S., & Kamel, M. I. (1998). Children experiencing violence II: Prevalence and determinants of corporal punishment in schools. *Child Abuse and Neglect: The International Journal, 22*(10), 975-985.

Zahn-Waxler, C. (1987, April). *Problem behaviors in young children.* Paper presented at the biennial meeting of the Society for Research in Child Development, Baltimore, Maryland.

Zigler, E., & Seitz, V. (1982). Determinants of development: Future research on socialization and personality development. In E. F. Zigler, M. E. Lamb, & I. L. Child (Eds.), *Socialization and personality development* (pp. 185-199). Oxford, UK: Oxford University Press.

Zito, J. M., Safer, D. J., dosReis, S., Gardner, J. F., Boles, M., & Lynch, R. (2000). Trends in the prescribing of psychotropic medications to preschoolers. *Journal of the American Medical Association, 283*(8), 1025-1030.

Also retrieved February 28, 2000, from the Internet: jama.ama-assn.org/issues/v283n8/full/joc91250.html

Zuckerman, D., & Zuckerman, B. (1985). Television's impact on children. *Pediatrics, 75,* 233-240.

Zwier, G., & Vaughan, G. M. (1984). Three ideological orientations in school vandalism research. *Review of Educational Research, 54*(2), 263-292.

Index

CORWIN PRESS

The Corwin Press logo—a raven striding across an open book—represents the happy union of courage and learning. We are a professional-level publisher of books and journals for K–12 educators, and we are committed to creating and providing resources that embody these qualities. Corwin's motto is "Success for All Learners."